Cultural Proficiency

A Manual for School Leaders

Randall B. Lindsey
Kikanza Nuri Robins
Raymond D. Terrell

CORWIN PRESS, INC.
A Sage Publications Company
Thousand Oaks, California

For information:

Corwin Press, Inc.
A Sage Publications Company
2455 Teller Road
Thousand Oaks, California 91320
E-mail: order@corwinpress.com

SAGE Publications Ltd.
6 Bonhill Street
London EC2A 4PU
United Kingdom

SAGE Publications India Pvt. Ltd.
M-32 Market
Greater Kailash I
New Delhi 110 048 India

Printed in the United States of America

Library of Congress Cataloging-in-Publication Data

Lindsey, Randall B.
  Cultural proficiency: A manual for school leaders/ by Randall
B. Lindsey, Kikanza Nuri Robins, and Raymond D. Terrell.
    p. cm.
  Includes bibliographical references and index.
  ISBN 0-8039-6762-4 (cloth: acid-free paper)
  ISBN 0-8039-6763-2 (pbk.: acid-free paper)
    1. Multicultural education—United States—Handbooks, manuals,
etc. 2. Educational sociology—United States—Handbooks, manuals,
etc. 3. School leadership—United States—Handbooks, manuals, etc.
I. Robins, Kikanza Nuri, 1950- II. Terrell, Raymond D. III. Title.
  LC1099.3 .L555 1999
  370.117'0973—dc21   98-51236

This book is printed on acid-free paper.

  00 01 02 03 04 10 9 8 7 6 5 4 3

Corwin Editorial Assistant: Julia Parnell
Production Editor: Denise Santoyo
Editorial Assistant: Patricia Zeman
Designer/Typesetter: Danielle Dillahunt
Cover Designer: Michelle Lee

Contents

Foreword

For years, education work that went under the label *multicultural* was well-intentioned, appropriate in orientation, but superficial. Culture was undefined. Rarely was there any grounding in the study of culture. Even as anthropologists were brought into the picture, our understanding of *diversity* was not enhanced much, given the extremely wide range of cultures that are a part of the American mosaic.

Not only was cultural understanding superficial, our understanding of pedagogy was not much better, especially valid pedagogy. Even now, it is hard to have a coherent dialogue about valid pedagogy. It is hard to separate the trivial from the substantial. It is hard to see how valid pedagogy makes a difference in everyday work. Yet powerful general approaches to teaching and learning exist and are well documented, and many demonstrations can be seen (e.g., Backler & Eakin, 1993; Ladson-Billings, 1994; Sizemore, 1982; Suzuki, 1987).

Valid pedagogy shows that, given a high quality of teaching and nurture, all children succeed in spite of IQ, poverty, crime and drug-ridden neighborhoods, and so forth. Simply put, ordinary teachers who are well prepared, motivated, and dedicated produce high achieving students. This production is not rocket science. With reasonably hard work and an appropriate focus, success is certain for all children (e.g., Spark, 1997).

Culture can be understood, and powerful pedagogy is within the grasp of well-prepared teachers. So why does success elude us, especially for so many poor, "minority" students? Simply put, a third factor complicates and obscures our view of both culture and pedagogy. It is politics. Teaching and learning in schools are the sites for power struggles. These sites are the places where hegemonic agenda are played out (e.g., Freire, 1970; Kozol, 1991; Oakes, 1985; Kohn, 1998). The intersection of these three things is the context within which teaching and learning take place. No understanding of school success and failure is possible in ignorance of how these things interact.

A sophisticated understanding of each of these three components, separately and in interaction with each other, is necessary to raise the level of professional dialogue, analysis, and professional practice.

This book is one in a small number that present clear voices on these matters. These authors plumb the deep structure of the diversity issue in education. They provide precise definitions of such things as culture and oppression. Moreover, they offer a wide array of anecdotal examples that have the ring of authenticity to them. The anecdotes alone are a rich source of stimulating materials guaranteed to launch meaningful dialogue. The anecdotes bring to life what would otherwise be dry and perhaps irrelevant talk about abstract things, things that are also likely to be decontextualized. Yet the authors weave these anecdotes skillfully into the text, giving it a robustness seldom found in educational literature.

As if this were not enough, the authors provide many activities suitable for staff development. Even veteran staff development leaders will find activities here to enrich their repertoires of best practice.

Culture is real and is a major element in all human interactions. Those who are blind to culture and diversity are blind to reality. Teaching power is also real. Those who are blind to that must improve their own competency. But above all, power and hegemony, the desire by some to dominate vulnerable groups, is alive and well. The ugly history of American apartheid (segregation) is but one example of how hegemony plays out in education and becomes embedded in structures of schooling, root and branch, from ideology to methodology to curriculum to assessment.

The theory and practice described and presented here challenge all to offer at least as much quality as the authors have shown. This is not to say that the discussion is closed. On the contrary, the book is open to even further development and exploration. For example, I am not at all persuaded that the "caste and immigrant" minority formulation is valid or useful in producing beneficial education. It is a theory that seems to be attractive to many. Hegemonic structures as I understand them do not make these nice distinctions. Further, the phenomenal success of so many schools with caste and minorities show beyond a doubt that high-quality school service can overcome, indeed has overcome, the status that may be accredited to the children. The problem is external to the child and family, not internal, even when the children and families are traumatized. We can never underestimate the nature of nurture as the source of school power.

This book is a major contribution to the education literature on diversity and pluralism in education. *Cultural proficiency*, as discussed here, contributes to the language of empowerment.

Asa G. Hilliard, III
Georgia State University

Preface

A s educators, we are used to trends. Every 3 to 5 years,
something new is presented that is supposed to be the
answer to all our professional nightmares. Some educational
innovations truly work; others simply make more work. About
30 years ago, educational sociologists and curriculum specialists
began writing about urban schools and the special demands
presented by students in our urban centers. Of course, *urban
school* was a euphemism for a school whose population was not
white middle class or better. The poor, the oppressed, the outcasts, and the castoffs lived in the urban cores of the United States.
Teachers and other educators needed to deal with them. Today,
the buzzword for this country's minorities, the women and men
who are the poor, the people of color, the gays and lesbians, and
the disabled, is *diversity*.

It has become politically correct to talk about issues of diversity. Anything that used to be labeled deprived, disadvantaged,
or different is now called diverse. In some schools, not much has
changed except the labels. We propose to talk not about how to
deal with diversity, but, rather how school leaders can respond
to issues arising from working with diverse populations. Diversity is as real as the chair in which you are sitting or this book that
you are holding. We do not need to discuss whether diversity is
an issue. Diversity is a neutral descriptor that lets you know that
the people around you are not all like you. What we propose to

do in this book is to help you develop positive and productive responses to the diversity in your school and community.

Cultural proficiency is a relatively new approach to diversity developed for work in mental health agencies. The *cultural proficiency model* provides a framework for individual and organizational change, both of which are necessary for systemic change. Cultural proficiency is the policies and practices of a school or the values and behaviors of an individual that enable the person or school to interact effectively in a culturally diverse environment. We introduce the cultural proficiency model to school leaders with examples relevant to school settings. This approach to the topic of diversity is easy to internalize. It provides a nonthreatening, comprehensive, systematic, and systemic structure. Its application is behavioral, focusing on individual performance as well as organizational policies and practices. Many schools and people have an aversion to dealing with their own issues related to equity, affirmative action, and diversity. We wrote this book because cultural proficiency provides a nonthreatening, comprehensive, systemic structure for school leaders addressing these issues.

Government agencies, including schools, continue to battle ineffectively with programs called affirmative action, multicultural curriculum projects, and diversity. Rarely do they deal with the underlying issues of class, caste, and culture that make diversity an issue in our country. As our society becomes increasingly diverse, so do our schools. In schools, the issues are complicated by student populations that change far more rapidly than the demographic profiles of the educators responsible for teaching them. Urban schools are heavily populated with students who historically have been underserved—African American, Latino, Caribbean, Native American, and students from low-income families. For these and many other related reasons, it is important for schools to address proactively the issues caused by the diversity of their communities, with approaches and programs designed not to fix but to change a system so that it is appropriate and responsive to the changes that have taken place among faculty, staff, students, and families. This book provides a structured and theoretically sound process for systematically addressing diversity in terms that enhance the educational opportunities of all students.

We are indebted to the work that others have done before us. John Ogbu, James Banks, Paolo Freire, Henry Giroux, Asa Hilliard,

Christine Sleeter, and Carol Gilligan have inspired us. Many other scholarly works remind us of all that can and cannot be presented in one volume. In this book, we therefore focus on the application of theory by contextualizing a model that has worked for the school practitioner in a variety of settings. This book is for formal and informal school leaders. It serves as a guide to analyzing schools and oneself as you plan, implement, and assess change. If we are going to create culturally proficient schools, the leaders at the school level must create them. So in addition to the practitioner, students in schools of education will find that the book complements their study of educational change, diversity, and emerging issues in education.

Culturally Proficient Schools uses examples from our work over the past 10 years in teaching school leaders how to adapt the cultural proficiency model to their unique situations. Our goal is to provide the reader with a strong conceptual understanding of cultural proficiency and to give specific, practical, field-tested applications of those same concepts. After reading *Culturally Proficient Schools*, you will have a model for assessing behavior and programs in schools. You will have a framework for implementing change within classrooms or schools or throughout districts. Additionally, you will have a comprehensive case study and structured exercises to use with your colleagues and staffs for helping them analyze and address the issues caused by diversity in schools.

We have adapted the theories of Terry Cross for use in schools and other agencies. In *Toward a Culturally Competent System of Care* (Cross, Bazron, Dennis, & Isaacs, 1989), he illustrates appropriate ways to meet the needs of culturally and ethnically diverse mental health clients.

Within the chapters of this book is an ongoing case study. In Chapter 2 we respond to the question, What is cultural proficiency? We define cultural proficiency in the context of guiding principles and essential elements that facilitate its application to the individual person as well as to the school setting. We then provide a historical context for the evolution of modern social policy and equity issues so you can better understand the dynamics of intergenerational issues among school faculties and between other groups. In Chapter 3, we describe the culturally proficient leader after summarizing the theories of leadership and organization that support systemic change in schools. In Chapters 4 and 5, we confront the reality that whenever there is change, there also exists the resistance to change. We discuss the change process in Chapter 4 and present activities for school leaders who are engaged as change agents. We devote Chapter 5 to understanding entitlement as a barrier to change. This type of change is the moral choice that informs personal responsibility and initiative.

We recognize there is no magic formula or silver bullet for improving schools. The magic (if there is any in this book) will happen when faculty uses the cultural proficiency model to guide inquiry and response to the issues caused by diversity within themselves and within their schools. This book

- Provides readers with guidelines for examining the school's policies and practices and their own values and behaviors using the principles of cultural proficiency
- Provides readers with a tool for categorizing a range of responses to differences—the *cultural proficiency continuum*
- Provides readers with performance-based criteria, the essential elements of cultural proficiency, to guide in planning for personal, professional, and curricular development
- Provides readers with descriptions of our work in schools, in the form of a case study, to illustrate each of the concepts we present

We recognize that some people will pick up this book and begin looking for quick solutions for their immediate problems, or for a step-by-step process guaranteed to work in any setting. They will be disappointed and will fail no matter what they try. Cultural proficiency is not a program supplement, nor is it a plug-and-play model. Schools that adapt the cultural proficiency model for responding to the issues of diversity make a commitment to change the culture of the school. The individual and the organization must grow and change to be culturally proficient. For that reason, it is important that we say what this book is not:

- It is not a collection of structured activities for random use in a staff development session. We do not recommend that readers skip the text and proceed to the activities in the Resources. Successful use of the activities is predicated on a thorough understanding of the underlying concepts in the cultural proficiency approach to diversity.

- It is not a collection of boilerplate school policies and practices such as those that regulate attendance, suspension, expulsion, and the identification of students for special services. We believe that schools are better served when school personnel and community members gather policies on their school, examine them along with the corollary practices, and recommend changes together, using the principles and essential elements of cultural proficiency as their guide.
- It is not a magic formula, a silver bullet, or a panacea. *You have to do the work.* Schools have been designed for some students to be successful. It will take great effort and hard work to make schools places where all students can be successful.

We are deeply grateful to several people who influenced this work. First, we thank Terry Cross (Cross et al., 1989) for his conceptualization of cultural proficiency. His pioneer work gave us the model by which to organize our experiences. It is the cultural proficiency model that has best supported school leaders as they design and implement programs that effectively serve all students.

Second, as authors, we are individually appreciative of each other. This book is an important benchmark in our 30 years of friendship, during which each of us has, in turn, been a teacher to and a learner from the others. Our friendship has become deeper and dearer during the creation of this book. We truly appreciate the love, friendship, and strong support from Delores Lindsey, who knew there were important lessons in this book project. We are deeply indebted to Shari Hatch, whose loving friendship nourished us as she blended our three voices into one with her editorial magic. We extend sincere gratitude and appreciation to our many students and clients who provided the data for our case study; who trusted us over the years as we introduced this model to them; and who proved over and over again that it is possible to create culturally proficient organizations. We are also grateful for the support of our editor, Alice Foster, and the comments from Francesina Jackson and Gwen Turner, whose suggestions were both pointed and pragmatic.

About the Authors

Randall B. Lindsey, PhD, is Professor and Chair of the Department of Education at the University of Redlands, Redlands, California. Prior to his position there, he served as chair of the department of educational administration and counseling in the school of education at California State University, Los Angeles. He has served as a junior and senior high school teacher of history and as an administrator in charge of desegregation and staff development programs. He has worked extensively with school districts as they plan for and experience changing populations.

Kikanza Nuri Robins, EdD, is an organizational development cosultant who specializes in cultural transformations. She has taught elementary and secondary school, and has worked with teachers as a professor and a staff development specialist. She has written articles and conducted workshops on language and culture, power and leadership, and spiritual development. She is the author of *Unspoken Visions: An Inner Journey* (1995).

Raymond D. Terrell, EdD, is the Distinguished Professional in Residence in the Department of Educational Leadership at Miami University in Oxford, Ohio. He has served as an elementary school principal in Hamilton, Ohio, after retiring as a professor of educational administration and dean of California State University's School of Education. He began his career as a public school teacher and administrator, and has over 25 years of professional experience with diversity and equity issues.

ONE

The Case

Presenting Rolling Meadows and Coolidge School Districts

The case used in this book is presented here in its entirety. In each chapter, you will find a portion of the case—sometimes at the beginning of the chapter, often integrated into the chapter—to illustrate points that we make. You may want to read the entire case now and then see how your analysis of it changes as you read each chapter. Another way to use the case study is to read it to familiarize yourself with the characters and the school districts, and then to reflect on the portion of the case that is presented in the chapter you are reading.

* * *

Rolling Meadows Unified School District has been getting some bad media coverage. One of the few black parents in the district, Barbara Latimer, an attorney, has been accusing some of the high school teachers of racism. Superintendent Hermon Watson is concerned and privately incensed. He has provided leadership for this district for the past 15 years, and he is not happy to have this kind of press coverage so close to his retirement. One of the reasons people live in this bedroom community is that it historically has been a stable, safe, family-oriented neighborhood in which to raise

1

kids. It has been a place where people move because the schools are good and people don't have to deal with the issues caused by integrated schools and neighborhoods. Rolling Meadows has its own business and civic center, and the majority of the population makes a long commute into the urban center for work.

Now the paper is quoting parents as saying, "We came out here to get away from these people. Now all they are doing is moving here and stirring up trouble."

Hermon shudders as he imagines his board members reading this over their morning coffee.

"We have handled every single incident that has occurred in this district. We don't have racist teachers, and we certainly are not a racist district," Hermon says as he reviews the *Morning Tribune* article with his cabinet.

"No one is perfect, and we have had only a few isolated incidents. We handle them discreetly, involve as few people as we can, and once it's handled, we don't speak of it again. My goal is that when we look at the faces in a classroom, or out across the commons area at lunchtime, we don't see colors, we just see kids."

Rolling Meadows is a growing suburban school district that has about 15,000 students in three high school clusters, a continuation high school, and an adult school. In 1988-89, the white student population of the district was 82%, with 4% Asian Pacific Islanders, 6% Latino, 2% African American, and 1% Native American. In 1996-97, the percentage of white students had declined to 52%, whereas the Asian Pacific Islander, Latino, African American, and Native American student populations maintained their relative growth. In contrast to the changing student demographics, the teaching force has been relatively stable since 1988-89. At that time, 90% of the teachers were white; in 1996-97, the percentage had decreased by only 5%.

Winston Alexander, the assistant superintendent for business, clears his throat. "I'm not sure, Hermon, but do you think that we ought to hire a consultant? It might look good right now to bring in some outside experts so they can tell the press what a good job we are doing."

"What a fabulous idea," exclaims Holly Kemp, the assistant superintendent for curriculum and instruction. "We just finished the RASC (Regional Association of Schools and Colleges) accreditation review, so our materials are in order. We could hire consultants to provide a cultural accreditation of some sort. We are not bad people, surely they will know that."

His cabinet rarely lets him down, Hermon muses. That is why they have been honored as a nationally distinguished district three times in the past 10 years. Aloud he says, "A cultural audit. Good idea. Winston and Holly, can the two of you put together an RFP (request for proposal) this week? Ask our attorney friend, Barbara Latimer, to give you some input. That should quiet her down for a while, and it will also let her know that we really mean to do well by her people."

"Winston, what kind of money can you find for this? We may need to dig deep to climb out of this hole."

* * *

The teachers at Rolling Meadows Middle School have heard that the district is going to hire some consultants to teach them to be racially sensitive. They are neither impressed nor pleased. Sitting in the teachers' lunchroom, they speak wistfully about when their own children attended the district, failing to acknowledge that the demographics have been changing dramatically. Their comments range in attitude from culturally destructive to culturally proficient:

"This is America, everyone should speak English."

"We didn't do anything to those people, why do we have to change?"

"This is America; they should be adapting to us."

"This is reverse discrimination."

"Why are we trying to fix something that's not broken?"

"I didn't know he was gay. He doesn't look gay to me."

"She catches well for a girl."

"I can't believe my Japanese boys only scored in the 80th percentile!"

"When I walk into a classroom, I do not see color or ability or gender, I only see children."

"We need a Korean vice principal to help us with the Korean students."

"We celebrate Cinco de Mayo and Martin Luther King's birthday. What holiday can we use for Native American Indians?"

"Let's get some consultants in here to help us out."

"To really understand student needs, we must disaggregate these test data."

"Let's look at the school calendar to make sure we don't schedule our potlucks during Ramadan, Ridvan, or Yom Kippur."[1]

"I believe that conflict is natural and normal; I'm glad we are learning how to do things differently when conflict occurs."

"Our goal for examining our school policy on student grouping must be to enhance student achievement."

* * *

On the other side of the county, Coolidge Unified District serves the families that live in the urban center where many Rolling Meadows adults work. The district is working with Jim Woodard, a diversity consultant. At the first staff development session, Jim explains the underlying principles that inform his approach to dealing with diversity. He hears some interesting comments as the teachers and administrators leave the session for the afternoon.

"I don't have a culture. I'm just a generic person. Heinz 57."

"Doesn't focusing on differences just make it harder for us to get along?"

"I don't see why they can't adjust like the rest of us did."

"All of us have suffered discrimination."

"You sure didn't sound black on the phone when we talked."

"I didn't know there were Chinese people over 6 feet tall."

"You are different, we're very comfortable with you."

"We would have more of your kind around if they were just like you."

"Why do they have to have a special program?"

"I think everyone should be given the same attention and information. That's fair."

* * *

The opinions of the faculty and administration at Rolling Meadows reflect the range of views in the community. Many believe that the school can be organized to provide a quality education for all students. A smaller and very vocal group, however, continually decries any changes that appear to lower standards and accuses the school and district administration of not supporting the school by getting tough with troublemakers. Members of this group believe that if the school returns to a well-defined tracking system that creates a vocational level for students who are not interested in learning, the needs of everyone will be served. They also believe that senior teachers should be given first choice for teaching courses.

This vocal minority among the veteran faculty continues to protest loudly the many changes occurring at the school. The faculty who have been at the school for fewer than 10 years tend to be much more culturally diverse. The principal is African American, and her administrative staff comprises a white male vice principal with two assistant principals who are a white female and a Latina. The white male has been an administrator at the school for 12 years, and the principal and assistant principals have been at the school 3 years or less. The principal and assistant principals are often perceived as affirmative action placements.

*　*　*

Leatha Harp, director of credentialing and certification in Coolidge School District, has gathered a small team of teachers and administrators who have agreed to serve on employment interview panels this school year to hire administrators for the district. They are reviewing anonymous comments written by other teachers and administrators when asked to discuss the type of leaders desired at Coolidge schools. The team has pulled out the comment sheets that reflect trends or themes in the responses. About the formal leaders in the district, they read:

- What that school needs is a strict disciplinarian so the kids will know who is in charge.
- The Latino kids need a Latino administrator so they can have a positive role model.
- Principals come and go, but I will always be here.
- This school is entirely too tough for a woman administrator!
- I may not agree with her, but I know where she stands.
- One thing I will have to give the principal, he sure does relate well to the parents.
- She may be an expert in instruction and supervision, but how can she evaluate my physics lesson?

"I had no idea the comments would be so personal," exclaims Brittney, one of the middle school teachers. "They sound so jaded."

"Oh, they are not all bad," says Leatha. "They tell us a lot about what people want in their leaders. Look at this pile of comments,"

Leatha continues. "They tell us a lot about where the nonformal leadership is in this district."

"What do you mean by nonformal?" asks Grace. The ink is still wet on her credential.

"Nonformal leaders are not officially appointed or chosen, but rather emerge spontaneously, based on the needs and aspirations of those who work in the school environment," explains Leatha.

"Nonformal leaders usually mean people such as teachers, aides, students, or parents. People who don't have official titles, but who have a lot of influence. Doris Harris, the director of the Citizens Human Relations Council, is a nonformal leader. She doesn't have such a high position, but everyone respects her and listens when she speaks. She is always at the district office and the board meetings. Look at these comments; they acknowledge the nonformal leadership we have in this district."

- That secretary has trained seven principals!
- As a new teacher, it is best to get on the good side of the secretary and the lead custodian.
- If you want to reach out to the parents, just tell Mr. Nguyen, Kim's father—he is well respected in this community.
- To include more bilingual parents in school governance, you may want to use the services of the aide in room 7; she has the ability to reach out well.
- The union representative is a very important member of the leadership council, but Mrs. Sandoval is the teacher to whom the others look for guidance.
- Why do the Athletic Boosters wield so much power?

* * *

Rolling Meadows Superintendent Watson recognizes that the demographics of the district are beginning to shift from being almost totally white to increasingly multicultural. He has gathered data on student achievement, openly noted the race-related fights at the high schools, and heard parents' complaints about the curriculum.

The RFP that his staff prepares seeks consultants to conduct a year-long cultural audit and needs assessment that taps into the views and beliefs of all sectors of the district—the educators, the staff, the students, and members of the community. Although he has not yet been introduced to the concept of cultural proficiency, he knows intuitively to move in this comprehensive direction and to involve many layers of the district administration for them to understand his vision for all students in the district. He uses his formal position to lead the district into this diversity needs assessment process.

*   *   *

In the urban center of the same county as Rolling Meadows, Coolidge Middle School Principal Richard Diaz is also ready to conduct a needs assessment. The school's student demographics have changed from virtually all African American to about one-fourth Latino in less than 5 years. Furthermore, his urban district includes about 70% Latino students. Among the many changes he has initiated at the middle school is to provide instruction in Spanish to all students. This not only provides those whose primary language is Spanish the opportunity to develop bilingual skills in both their native tongue and their new language (English), but it also offers native English speakers the chance to learn Spanish, to prepare to function in multilingual settings as teenagers and adults. His vision helps African American students learn about the lifestyles of the Spanish-speaking students, and it mitigates any pressures that could result from having two languages spoken in the school.

*   *   *

Winston Alexander, Rolling Meadows assistant superintendent for business, is reviewing the proposals he has received in response to the RFP and is learning a lot. He gets some information from the specific responses to the questions the RFP team proposes, but the team gleans even more insight from the underlying values of the consultants. It is easy to discern what they believe from the way they present themselves and in the extra materials they included. Right now he muses over two ideas:

- No nation has ever undertaken to provide universal education for as broad a spectrum of social class and ethnic or racial groups as has the United States.

- We are more successful at education than any nation in the world today, but our development of a de facto caste system has created great inequities. We are at a point in history where we must heed the warning to avoid creating "two societies, separate and unequal" (Riot Commission, 1968).

At Coolidge Middle School, Derek effectively teaches children from diverse ethnic and socioeconomic backgrounds, but down the hall, Brittney, a second-year teacher, is unsuccessful with and unhappy about having to teach "that kind of child," referring to various children from the local community. DeLois, Kareem, and several other teachers here organize their students by reading levels, continuously moving children to the next highest reading level as they progress through the year. By June, their top groups are quite large. On the other hand, Brittney is among the many other teachers in the school who organize reading levels at the beginning of the year and keep the students in the same groups all year long, regardless of how much individual students progress.

In the faculty meeting room, Fernando, the vice principal of curriculum and climate, writes on the board, "That men do not learn very much from the lessons of history is the most important of all the lessons that history has to teach. Aldous Huxley, 1959."

"There he goes again," Harvey whispers to Lane. Fernando has developed a mantra of change and a rallying cry for the new order of things he is trying to establish at Coolidge Middle School. He knows that one speech, one memo, or one staff meeting will not do it. Every time the faculty and staff members see him, Fernando talks about change and what it will mean for whomever he is addressing, as well as how it will affect the students and the school's community.

"These diversity staff development meetings are a waste of time," Harvey continues. "No one's going to change. I've been here for 17 years, and I've seen it all. I have tenure, so I'll just sit tight. These VPs are only here until they get a promotion. Each one brings his or her own program, and each program leaves with the VP. If I wait long enough, I won't have to do a thing."

Across the room, DeLois and Kareem are eagerly taking notes. "I wish I had taken more history courses when I was in college," DeLois sighs. "I'm sure that I could be more effective if I had a stronger historical foundation for what we are doing."

"We're not here to teach history, we're here to teach kids," Kareem retorts. "I wish he would just tell us more about this cultural proficiency model so I can figure out what I have to do in my classroom."

"You're right," Ellie pipes in, "Fernando just needs to mandate what he wants done. Understanding history is not going to change some of the bigots in this room."

* * *

DeLois is looking at her Heroes and Holidays calendar, which she has been so proud of. At the staff development session today, she learned that her approach of selecting one month each year to focus on a particular ethnic group is leading to cultural incapacity. She now understands that learning to say "Happy New Year" in Chinese and reading a story about Cesar Chavez will not significantly change the way the students interact with each other on the playground, and it will probably do nothing to raise scores on standardized tests. It has taken her years to collect costumes, recipes, and thousands of pictures—pictures of Chinese babies, African children, and families in the Brazilian rain forest. Now, as she packs them away, DeLois wonders how many parents she insulted by pointing proudly to the pictures saying, "We have a lesson on your people, so your child will be comfortable in our classroom." Sighing deeply, DeLois places the box on the shelf.

Kareem walks into the classroom and notices DeLois's red-rimmed eyes. "Why are you so down? I thought you were gung ho on this cultural proficiency thing. You even volunteered to chair the policy examination committee."

"Well, I'm a little sad, Kareem. I hate to think that everything I've been doing all these years has been a waste."

"No, it hasn't been a waste. I never really understood your party approach to diversity, but I have noticed that you treat every child with respect, compassion, and the expectation that they will achieve. Then you make sure that they do by adjusting your style to their needs and abilities. I think that reflects your cultural proficiency more than this calendar and those recipes do."

"Thanks, Kareem," DeLois sniffs. "I guess this certificate of appreciation from the principal does say that some people noticed I was trying."

* * *

Principal Dina Turner is conducting a meeting with her site council. "We are at the midpoint of our year, and our plan specifies that we are to assess our progress by examining our benchmarks. As you recall, our goals for this year were for schoolwide academic improvement in reading and for learning more about our interaction patterns with students."

Bobby, one of her consistently unhappy teachers, replies, "You know, I am all for academic improvement, but I still don't see how it is related to having a teacher observing me in my classroom."

Another teacher, Celeste, speaks up in Dina's defense. "I am not sure that I can agree with you. I have noticed that the school-wide focus on reading has made it easier to talk with my students about the recreational benefits of reading."

Grace Ishmael, a very active parent in the district, adds, "That is a good point! Just this weekend my son asked if I didn't think that we watched way too much television. I hated to admit it, but he is right. I was just wondering how parents who are not members of the site council are reacting."

Dina says, "Obviously I am very supportive of our reading initiative. I am also deeply committed to our continued study of student-teacher interactions. Has anyone had the occasion to apply any of the research on teacher expectations in their class-rooms?"

"Yes, I have," says Celeste. "You know, Bobby, I am confident that I am a good teacher, but those activities are really giving me insights to some of my blind spots. I am beginning to see how unintended behaviors can be so harmful!"

"What occurs to me," adds Dina, "is that if these behaviors occur between students and teachers, they must occur among adults too. I shudder at the thought!"

Grace has an idea. "You know, we may want to consider some of that training for parents. From what you are saying, it may be very enlightening, possibly a little uncomfortable, but very worthwhile."

"I do want to speak to the issue of discomfort," Dina replies. "Most teachers do not find the process uncomfortable. I believe if everyone sees themselves as students and are willing to commit the energy it takes to walk this avenue to improvement, we will all grow and our kids will really benefit. And, I agree, it would be good for this group too. It would be an excellent topic for training all our parents."

* * *

"We didn't do anything to those people, why do we have to change?"

"This is America; they should be adapting to us."

"This is reverse discrimination."

"Why are we trying to fix something that's not broken?"

* * *

In Coolidge District, after principals Steve Petrossian, Richard Diaz, and Dina Turner hear that the board of education votes not to embrace cultural proficiency as a district policy, these administrators decide to make the guiding principles of cultural proficiency (see Chapter 2) their own value base for decision making. They regularly meet to offer one another support and encouragement in implementing their goals for cultural proficiency.

To move his school toward cultural proficiency, Steve carefully studies the essential elements of cultural proficiency (see Chapter 2), then decides to start with the element valuing diversity because many of his staff members fervently resist any change. Their practices in the past have ranged from cultural incapacity to cultural blindness. Nonetheless, Steve has a couple of teachers (e.g., DeLois and Kareem) who truly value diversity and who are willing to chair committees that will develop ideas for manifesting a value for diversity on the campus.

Given the adamant resistance of his staff, Steve spends more time in the ending phase of managing transition (see Table 4.2). He has to make a case for change by showing the resisters how past behaviors have damaged the students, the school's relationships with the community, and the school's reputation in the district. He then has to convince his teachers that the proposed change is integral to the school program, not just a supplement to it. After Steve implements the plan for integrating this element into his school system, he consults with faculty and staff to select another element for focus.

Richard Diaz, a middle school principal, is pleased to report that despite several false starts, he finally has had a number of celebrations as part of the food and fiestas program. Richard knows that this is only a superficial beginning, but it is all he can motivate his people to do. Initially, many of Richard's staff members resisted

change because they perceived that change meant that they had done something wrong or that their ideas and programs were no longer valued. After a conversation with his colleagues, facilitated by the diversity consultant, all together have been seeking new ways to address the issues of diversity. All participants are proud of what they are doing, and they are eager to do even more.

Richard knows that social events like the food and fiestas program are at best precompetent, but he knows that to be successful he has to create an environment where the faculty experience success. He makes a mental note to move quickly to more substantive activities.

Dina, the principal at the high school, has had a terrible year and is now facing some court recriminations. She is going to start with the element managing the dynamics of difference. Some of Dina's resisters declare that because they were not directly involved in any of the conflicts leading to the court battles, they should not be punished by having to attend any workshops. Dina overcomes the resistance by reframing the situation. She points out that current activities are not punishment, they are simply a response to changes in the school's culture that, heretofore, have not been acknowledged well. This is an opportunity to show students and parents what good teachers they are and how well they respond to their students' needs. They all need to learn how to recognize conflicts caused by cultural differences, and they all need to find appropriate ways to respond to them. Like Steve, Dina implements a plan for integrating this element into the school's culture and then works with faculty and staff to choose the next element on which to focus.

* * *

Coolidge High School continues to be among the schools in the district and region that earn top academic honors. The advanced placement classes have fewer than 10% African American and Latino students. In the last 5 years, the Title I population has increased from 5% to 35%. In that same time period, the English as a second language (ESL) classes have increased from serving less than 2% of the student population to serving slightly more than 35% of the student population. There have been two resulting effects of these trends. The first has been decreased sections of honors classes and a dramatic increase in remedial and heterogeneous classes. The heterogeneous classes in English and social studies were created to overcome criticism about the negative effect of tracking; however, placement in mathematics and science classes has served to create levels among the English and social studies classes.

The second effect of the demographic changes has been that the school's standardized test scores have steadily declined and have given the impression to the local media that the quality of education at the school has deteriorated. Teachers still have an interest in a traditional academic approach to curriculum. They also place a high value on a tracked system, in which the highest achievers are allowed to move at an accelerated rate.

The extracurricular programs of the school, except for football and basketball, tend to be associated with cultural groups. Though the sports program is nominally integrated, swimming is perceived to be a white sport, wrestling a Latino sport, track an African American sport, and tennis an Asian Pacific Islander sport. Student government represents the demographic profile of the school, but most of the clubs and other organizations are predominated by one cultural group. Of the major cultural groups at the school, Latino students participate least in clubs and other organizations. In recent years, there has been tension among the groups. Some fights and retaliatory attacks have received wide coverage in the newspaper.

Bill Fayette, assistant superintendent of curriculum and instruction at Coolidge, has organized inservice training sessions for faculty on cultural sensitivity that have focused on the contributions of African Americans, Latinos, and Asian Pacific Islanders. As a result, a few teachers have organized culture clubs for students, and they are talking about developing elective ethnic studies courses.

* * *

The Rolling Meadows consultants are presenting to Superintendent Watson's cabinet, and Holly, the assistant superintendent of curriculum and instruction, is not so sure they really understand the situation at Rolling Meadows because she hasn't seen any of these problems.

They say, "Throughout U.S. educational history, students have been taught little to nothing about the caste system in this country and precious little about U.S. citizens of lower castes. In recent decades, however, most textbooks and school curricula have inserted some materials and lessons mentioning women and people of color, although these insertions have generally been few and segregated from the sweep of U.S. history. Acknowledgment of African Americans is generally limited to scant lessons on slavery, the celebration of Dr. King's birthday, and observances of black history month in February. Lessons about Native American Indians often range from highlighting their nobility to underscoring their savagery; usually, their only significant role is to attend the first Thanksgiving. Lessons about Latinos are frequently relegated to music, dance, and a lesson about Cesar Chavez, if they are mentioned at all outside of the southwestern United States. Students learn about Asians as the celebrants of Chinese New Year, the sneaky attackers at Pearl Harbor, and the reluctant recipients of our 'help' during the Korean and Vietnam Wars. Lessons about women often resort to the great woman approach, focusing on a few heroic individuals, rather than the historic and continuing role of women in the United States. These discrete lessons lead to the objectification and invisibility of girls and children of color."

* * *

One of the consultants turns to a page on his flip chart with these quotations:

"If we are celebrating diversity, why don't we have celebrations like white history month?"

"The teacher wrote on my child's paper that she didn't understand the black inner-city experience. This child has never lived in the inner city! Her father is a chemist and I am a lawyer. Her teacher knows we are a middle-class family."

"These immigrant students don't even have magazines and books in their homes. They are at a tremendous disadvantage when compared to the other students."

After giving the cabinet a chance to reflect on the effect of these statements, the consultant remarks, "Each of these comments assumes that entitled students are the standard of measure for other students. In the first comment, it is not recognized that most traditional school curricula celebrate the dominant culture daily. The second illustration shows the lack of awareness of the relationship of social class to ethnic culture. The last quote reflects the assumption that the speaker knows what is in students' homes and that students with books and magazines read them!"

* * *

As a young teacher of social studies, Evan Brown was aware of being ill prepared to provide for the black students in his classroom even before coming to Coolidge High School. To remedy that inadequacy, he enrolled in a degree program at a major midwestern university and took coursework on the history of the U.S. Negro. It did not take him long to identify the gaps in his undergraduate education. Moreover, he realized quickly that his white students would also benefit from this material, while at the same time he continued to puzzle many of his Euro-American professors and colleagues. They did not understand why a bright young white man with a fairly secure future would want to waste his time this way.

Evan also noticed the degree to which entitlement had affected his own perceptions. First, his prior education provided almost no information on black history, thereby rendering it invisible, discounted entirely. Second, his original motivation to enroll in the courses, which had been to prepare himself to teach black students, changed with his realization that such information is of benefit to all students.

In 1968, he moved to California to continue his teaching career and to have two more startling experiences that increased his cultural proficiency. When he taught students of Mexican and Portuguese descent for the first time, he experienced the same sense of inadequacy he had felt in his midwestern classroom. Then, in discussing curricular content with colleagues, he was shocked to learn that U.S. citizens of Japanese ancestry had been incarcerated in U.S. relocation camps during World War II. His shock and anger were derived from two sources: (1) that his own country could do such a thing to its own citizens, and (2) that he had earned degrees in social studies from two reputable universities yet had no knowledge of this event.

* * *

During an inservice session on cultural proficiency at the Coolidge District, Jim Woodard, the consultant, overhears this conversation between European American Principal Steve Petrossian and Puerto Rican Vice Principal Fernando Rios:

Steve says, "You know, this activity in determining how prejudice differs from racism or sexism gives me some new information.

I had never considered the concept of power; it just never occurred to me. Let me ask you this, and you tell me what it is: One of my African American teachers said that one of our students is 'a good athlete for a white boy.' Now isn't that racism?"

"Steve," Fernando replies, "let me get this straight: You have been on this planet for decades, and you have never thought about the power that white people have in this country?"

Steve is defensive. "Hey, why attack me? I'm being straight with you. Power is something I've just never considered. Shoot, just because I'm white doesn't mean that I have power. Besides, you haven't answered my question. Isn't my story an example of racism?"

Jim responds to Steve. "No, it isn't. Although his story illustrates ethnocentric use of a stereotype, the teacher in your story lacks the power to institutionalize his belief."

Jim continues, addressing the whole group. "The story also shows Steve's lack of awareness of—and wish to deny—his own entitlement. The teacher in Steve's story was not reinforcing or perpetuating institutional racism, which affects every single person and has grave social consequences no matter whether it is recognized or acknowledged. More often than not, people who are not directly affected by oppression fail to understand when cultural groups speak out about their experiences. This failure is frequently translated into the egocentric view . . ."

Fernando interrupts: "Yeah, they say, 'If I didn't experience the oppression, or witness it, then you must be overreacting.' "

Jim goes on, "If we are to create an effectively functioning society—and, by extension, a school system that is culturally proficient—we must find ways to address issues of entitlement. By doing so, we can minimize gaps in the education of our educators that perpetuate their lack of awareness and their denial of their own empowerment."

* * *

At Coolidge Middle School this conversation takes place in the parking lot after a session with Consultant Jim Woodard.

Teacher DeLois says, "I am really enjoying this session on cultural proficiency. I can see where I can use a lot of this information to prepare the girls and Latinos in my classes to assume a responsible role in society."

Dakota Blaine, the dean of discipline, lashes back, "Are you for real? I would like you and this 'cultural expert' to spend a day in my office. All I deal with is the scum of this school. If they were in your classroom, you would know why those people are so behind in school."

Ellie, another teacher, chimes in. "Let me tell you a thing or two. First, if you think the girls and the Mexicans are the ones who need help, you are in worse shape than you know. The true scum in this school are the professional educators who do not see students when they come to their office. All you see is the color of their skin and you judge the kids and their families in the same way."

* * *

Consider a discussion that takes place among some teachers at Coolidge High School.

"I have been at this school for 17 years, and have I seen some changes!" says Michelle.

"Like what?" Bobby queries.

"Well, first of all," Michelle responds, "when I first came here, this was a nice, stable, working-class community where the parents wanted their children to have more than they did. Sure we had problems, but nothing like today."

"Yeah," Lee joins in, "then 14 years ago, about the same time the forced busing started, the school became all black in no time at all!"

"And?" Bobby challenges.

"What do you mean, 'And'?" Lee was getting annoyed. "You know exactly 'and what.' That was when our test scores dropped, drug problems began, and the school became one more ghetto nightmare. And I'm not a racist, these are just facts!"

Michelle tries to clarify their position. "Of course we're not racist. At least now the demographics are on our side. With the Asian students we have now, parents see to it that their kids study, and the Latino kids, they keep their gang trouble out of the school and in their own neighborhoods."

* * *

In less than 10 years, Rolling Meadows has changed from almost totally white to majority Cuban, most of whom are first generation immigrants, with Armenian, Korean, and white students having comparable numbers. After several years of declining test scores, rapid student growth (from 1,000 to 2,000 students, partly from the addition of the ninth grade), and increasing student-to-student conflicts, the principal of several years was forced into retirement. This very insular district rarely hired administrators from outside, but in this case, it went outside the district and hired the district's first woman, Julie Scales, who is also the first African American high school principal. She had served as an assistant principal in another state, but this is her first principalship. In the first 2 years, there was little evidence that anyone mentored her or showed her the "Rolling Meadows way of doing business." Another pressure on Julie was that last year Rolling Meadows was given only partial accreditation from the regional accrediting agency, a blow to the egos in the district and the community. It was only after a consultant spent 6 days on campus interviewing teachers, students, aides, administrators, and parents and issued a report of his findings that faculty confronted the fact that the mission of the school had changed. It had been a school that "prepared students for college"; now it is a school that also has to prepare students to become citizens of this country.

NOTE

1. These are the holidays of the Muslim, Baha'i and Jewish faiths, respectively, that require the faithful to fast during the day. Ramadan and Ridvan last for several weeks, so your Muslim and Baha'i colleagues and students may be at school while fasting.

TWO

What Is Cultural Proficiency?

Rolling Meadows Unified School District has been getting some bad media coverage. One of the few black parents in the district, Barbara Latimer, an attorney, has been accusing some of the high school teachers of racism. Superintendent Hermon Watson is concerned and privately incensed. He has provided leadership for this district for the past 15 years, and he is not happy to have this kind of press coverage so close to his retirement. One of the reasons people live in this bedroom community is that it historically has been a stable, safe, family-oriented neighborhood in which to raise kids. It has been a place where people move because the schools are good and people do not have to deal with the issues caused by integrated schools and neighborhoods. Rolling Meadows has its own business and civic center, and the majority of the population makes a long commute into the urban center for work.

Now the paper is quoting parents as saying, "We came out here to get away from these people. Now all they are doing is moving here and stirring up trouble."

Hermon shudders as he imagines his board members reading this over their morning coffee.

"We have handled every single incident that has occurred in this district. We don't have racist teachers, and we certainly are not a racist district," Hermon says as he reviews the *Morning Tribune* article with his cabinet.

"No one is perfect, and we have had only a few isolated incidents. We handle them discreetly, involve as few people as we can, and once it's handled, we don't speak of it again. My goal is that when we look at the faces in a classroom, or out across the commons area at lunchtime, we don't see colors, we just see kids."

Rolling Meadows is a growing suburban school district that has about 15,000 students in three high school clusters, a continuation high school, and an adult school. In 1988-89, the white student population of the district was 82%, with 4% Asian Pacific Islanders, 6% Latino, 2% African American, and 1% Native American. In 1996-97, the percentage of white students had declined to 52%, whereas the Asian Pacific Islander, Latino, African American, and Native American student populations maintained their relative growth. In contrast to the changing student demographics, the teaching force has been relatively stable since 1988-89. At that time, 90% of the teachers were white; in 1996-97, the percentage had decreased by only 5%.

Winston Alexander, the assistant superintendent for business, clears his throat. "I'm not sure, Hermon, but do you think that we ought to hire a consultant? It might look good right now to bring in some outside experts so they can tell the press what a good job we are doing."

"What a fabulous idea," exclaims Holly Kemp, the assistant superintendent for curriculum and instruction. "We just finished the RASC (Regional Association of Schools and Colleges) accreditation review, so our materials are in order. We could hire consultants to provide a cultural accreditation of some sort. We are not bad people, surely they will know that."

His cabinet rarely lets him down, Hermon muses. That is why they have been honored as a nationally distinguished district three times in the past 10 years. Aloud he says, "A cultural audit. Good idea. Winston and Holly, can the two of you put together an RFP (request for proposal) this week? Ask our attorney friend, Barbara Latimer, to give you some input. That should quiet her down for a while and it will also let her know that we really mean to do well by her people."

JUST ANOTHER EDUCATION TREND?

Every few years, some new process, concept, reform, or innovation is touted as the magic cure-all that will remedy whatever ails the profession—followed by disappointment that many ailments continue to plague us. Often, we educators are as baffled by—and perhaps impatient with—these perpetual shifts (and their accompanying array of dazzling new terminology) as are members of the wider community. One of the many contemporary trends in education centers on finding ways to appreciate

Cultural proficiency is the policies and practices of an organization or the values and behaviors of an individual that enable that agency or person to interact effectively in a culturally diverse environment. Cultural proficiency is reflected in the way an organization treats its employees, its clients, and its community.

Figure 2.1. Cultural Proficiency

the rich differences among our students. Because of our hard-earned skepticism, many of us wonder how—or even whether—the previous decade's focus on *multiculturalism* really differs from this decade's emphasis on *diversity*. As this book shows, however, this shift is not merely a superficial, overrated change in terminology but a much-needed, profound change in perspective. Unlike the trend toward multiculturalism, which focused narrowly on students' ethnic and racial differences, the shift toward diversity responds to societal trends urging us to take a broader approach to addressing equity issues, encompassing a wide range of differences, including race, class, ethnicity, gender, sexual orientation, and physical and sensory abilities across students.

When discussing terminology related to diversity, another term frequently comes to the surface: *political correctness*. This book presents an approach to addressing diversity issues that goes beyond political correctness. In fact, political correctness yields only superficial changes rather than profound ones because the underlying intentions of such an outlook may not always be sincere. We encourage educators to seek cultural proficiency rather than political correctness. Culturally proficient responses may appear similar to politically correct ones at first glance, but on closer inspection, they reveal greater depth of knowledge, introspection, and sincere intent than may be found in politically correct responses. The sincere intent underlying cultural proficiency (Figure 2.1) reflects a firm belief that response to diversity is both necessary and good.

Culturally proficient educators recognize that *culture* involves far more than ethnic or racial differences. They demonstrate an understanding of the cacophony of diverse cultures each person experiences in the school setting. Although they accept that they will not necessarily have intimate knowledge about each of the cultures represented in a classroom, school, or district, they recognize their need to learn more continually. They develop a conscious awareness of the culture of their communities, districts, or schools, and they understand that each has a powerful influence on the educators, students, parents, and community associated with that school or district. There are six points along the cultural proficiency continuum that indicate unique ways of seeing and responding to difference:

- Cultural destructiveness: The elimination of other people's cultures
- Cultural incapacity: Belief in the superiority of one's culture and behavior that disempowers another's culture
- Cultural blindness: Acting as if the cultural differences you see do not matter or not recognizing that there are differences among and between cultures
- Cultural precompetence: Awareness of the limitations of one's skills or an organization's practices when interacting with other cultural groups
- Cultural competence: Interacting with other cultural groups using the five essential elements of cultural proficiency as the standard for individual behavior and school practices: acceptance and respect for difference; ongoing assessment of one's own and the organization's culture; attention to the dynamics of difference; continuous expansion of cultural knowledge and resources; and the adaptation of one's values and behaviors and the organization's policies and practices
- Cultural proficiency: Esteeming culture; knowing how to learn about individual and organizational culture; interacting effectively in a variety of cultural environments

What makes this book different from other books on diversity? We use the cultural proficiency model as the foundation for addressing the issue of differences in schools. In this chapter, we discuss the following:

- The cultural proficiency model for addressing issues of diversity
- The definition of culture and its various manifestations
- The cultural proficiency continuum
- The essential elements of cultural proficiency
- The guiding principles of cultural proficiency

Subsequent chapters look specifically at culturally proficient leadership, barriers to changing for cultural proficiency, and the issue of entitlement. The final chapter addresses the all-important questions: So now what? What do you do with the information? How do you start to create a culturally proficient environment for your classroom, school, or district?

WHAT'S IN IT FOR US?

Why should educators respond to issues of diversity? Because effective responses to diversity target several mutually interactive goals that educators care deeply about. Such responses

- Enhance students' ability to learn and teachers' ability to teach
- Prepare students to find their own places in the global community they will enter when they leave our school communities
- Promote positive community relations and lead to outstanding citizenship
- Foster effective leadership

Learning and Teaching Effectively

Addressing the many complex issues associated with diversity is tough under any circumstances. Such issues become even more complex in school settings with large numbers of students whose experiences reflect diverse races, socioeconomic classes, languages, and cultures, as well as differing genders and sexual orientations. Sometimes, the challenge may seem so daunting as to be impossible. We must rise to the challenge, however, if we are to teach our students effectively. For one thing, for our students to learn what we have to offer, they must feel fully appreciated as individuals, within the context of their own distinctive cultural, racial, linguistic, and socioeconomic backgrounds, and with their own particular gender, sexual orientation, and sensory and physical abilities. For another, we need to address issues of diversity to respond sensitively to the needs of our students to facilitate their learning. In addition, we need to address issues of diversity to provide mutual support to one another so that each of us feels understood and appreciated.

Living in a Global Community

Within the last decade or so, it has become increasingly apparent that issues of diversity play a vital role in the economic and political life of our nation. Our ability to understand and appreciate diverse peoples both within our borders and across them profoundly affects our ability to flourish in the global economy and the world political community. We must prepare our children to function well and to interact effectively with the richly diverse people of the world. To do so, we must start by helping them address issues of diversity in each of our school and home communities. If we succeed, our educational programs will enable students to play vital roles wherever they go in our global community. As U.S.[1] business people have been learning, our nation's economic and political well-being depends on our ability to foster this appreciation of diversity. If we are to prepare our future adults for this challenge, we must commit ourselves to addressing issues of diversity in our schools effectively.

Participating in the Community

As educators, we play a key role in enhancing the relationship between the school and the community, both as individuals and as participants in schoolwide and districtwide decisions. As we respond to issues of diversity, we can change policies and practices that may negatively affect community members whose ethnicity, gender, age, sexual orientation, language, or ability differs from those of school leaders. A diversity program provides tools for examining your school and district to eliminate inappropriate policies, procedures, and practices that create negative outcomes for many students.

Providing Leadership

Through a successful diversity program, you can improve staff and student morale by improving the effectiveness of communication, reducing complaints, and creating a more comfortable and pleasing climate for persons in the school. As an educational leader, you can learn concepts and skills that you can translate into new initiatives, curricula, programs, and activities that will enrich school life for all students and staff. As greater awareness and understanding develop in schools, so too will the awareness and understanding of the larger community be expanded. We believe that very few of us actually intend to hurt other people. Diversity programs provide all of us with the information and skills we need to help us avoid unintentional slights or hurts and improve the quality of life for our school and home communities.

CULTURAL PROFICIENCY: WHAT IS IT?

Clearly, educators need some means of addressing cultural diversity. In our experience, the most effective and productive approach to addressing cultural diversity within schools is a model known as *cultural proficiency*. A culturally proficient environment acknowledges and responds to both individual and group differences. In a culturally proficient school, the educators and students know they are valued, and they involve community members in the school to facilitate their own cultural understanding. The culture of the school promotes inclusiveness and institutionalizes processes for learning about differences and responding appropriately to differences. Rather than lamenting "Why can't *they* be like *us*?" teachers and students welcome and create opportunities to understand who they are as individuals better while learning how to interact positively with people who differ from themselves.

The cultural proficiency model uses an inside-out approach that focuses first on those of us who are insiders to the school, encouraging us to reflect on our own individual understandings and values. It thereby relieves those identified as outsiders, the members of the excluded groups, from the responsibility of doing all the adapting. The cultural proficiency approach to diversity surprises many people, who expect a diversity program to teach them about other people, not about themselves. This inside-out approach acknowledges and validates the current values and feelings of people, encouraging change without threatening people's feelings of worth.

The cultural proficiency approach prizes individuals but focuses chiefly on the school's culture, which has a life force beyond the individuals within the school. This focus removes the need both to place blame on individuals and to induce feelings of guilt. The process involves all members of the school community in determining how to align policies, practices, and procedures to achieve cultural proficiency. Because all the participants are deeply involved in the developmental process, there is broader-based ownership, making it easier to commit to change. This approach attacks the problems caused by the diversification of students, faculty, and staff at a systemic level.

Building cultural proficiency requires informed and dedicated faculty and staff, committed and involved leadership, and time. Educators cannot be sent to training for 2 days and be expected to return with solutions to all the equity issues in their school. For instance, this model does *not* involve the use of simple checklists for identifying culturally significant characteristics of individuals, which may be politically appropriate but socially and educationally meaningless. The transformation to cultural proficiency requires time to think, reflect, assess, decide, and change. To become culturally proficient, educators participate actively in work sessions, contributing their distinctive ideas, beliefs, feelings, and perceptions. Consequently, their contributions involve them deeply in the process and make it easier for them to commit to change.

If you are truly committed to embracing diversity, you can use the cultural proficiency model to achieve diversity at a systemic level. The culturally proficient school district closes the door on tokenism and stops the revolving door through which highly competent, motivated people enter briefly and exit quickly because they have not been adequately integrated into the school's culture. Culturally proficient educators can confidently deliver education knowing that their students genuinely want it, and can readily receive it without having their cultural connections denied, offended, or threatened. Culturally proficient educators can also be sure that their community perceives them as a positive, contributing force that substantively enhances the community's image and the school's position in it.

WHAT IS CULTURE?

To become culturally proficient, you may need to be willing to expand your conceptual paradigm for *culture* to encompass everything that people believe and everything that they do that identifies them as members of a group and distinguishes that group from other groups. To most people, diversity connotes racial and ethnic differences. *Racial and ethnic cultures* are tied to a common history, ancestry, and geographic origin. In addition, each of us identifies with the culture of our own gender and sexual orientation; these are influenced by the wider culture's expectations and roles for each gender and sexual orientation, as well as the aspects of these cultures that are self-determined. In addition, organizational, occupational, and social cultures shape people's values and affect their communications. For instance, *social cultures* are groups of people who share a common interest or activity (e.g., jogging, volunteer work, arts and crafts). *Occupational cultures* are based on involvement in a common vocation (e.g., teachers, administrators, lawyers, and accountants—each group evokes an image). Dress, the language used, and what people believe in are all aspects of occupational culture. People who work for the same school or district are members of an *organizational culture.* They share values of the larger district but differ from educators in other schools and offices in the district.

In 1871, British anthropologist Edward Burnett Tylor defined *culture* as "that complex whole which includes knowledge, beliefs, art, law, morals, customs and any other capabilities and habits acquired by a member of society." Culture is everything you believe and everything you do that enables you to identify with people who are like you and that distinguishes you from people who differ from you. Culture is about groupness. A culture is a group of people identified by their shared history, values, and patterns of behavior. Culture provides parameters for daily living. The purpose of a culture is to assist people who are members of a group to know what the rules for acceptable behavior are and to provide consistency and predictability in everyday actions. These rules are called *cultural expectations.* The cultural expectations for a group assist in screening outsiders and controlling insiders, thus providing the basis for a group to sustain itself. When people think of culture, they often think only in terms of *ethnic culture* and the behaviors associated with people who look different. Ethnic culture is related to ancestral heritage and geography, common history, and, to some degree, physical appearance. Ethnic cultural groups are commonly called *racial groups. Race* is a concept developed by social scientists that was misinterpreted and popularized by eugenicists and social Darwinists in the 19th century in an attempt to characterize people by their physical features and to use those differences societally to justify the subjugation of people of color and perpetuate the dominance of the white race.

In this book, we use the term *race* to denote the large groups of people distinguished from one another by their physical appearances. These groups are people of African descent (blacks), people of European descent (whites), Asian Pacific Islanders, Native Americans, and Hispanics or Latinos/Latinas. Clearly, these groupings exclude a large number of people. Such groupings do not speak to the widespread migration and miscegenation that has created what we call mixed-race, biracial, or multiracial groups. For instance, what should we call the people of African descent who live in Central and South America and who speak Spanish? Are they Hispanic or of African descent? What about white South Africans? Are they Africans of European descent? Racial terminology inadequately names the different racially defined ethnic groups. It would seem to be more functional for us to develop ways of identifying, interacting with, and responding to any persons who are different in ways that demonstrate a value for human dignity.

Does it really make much of a difference what names we call one another, whether we use racial, cultural, or other kinds of names? Yes. To grasp this importance, simply think about your own name and the names of your children or other family members. Clearly, names mean a great deal to us. U.S. citizens are not alone in attaching deep meaning to names: Across cultures, the naming process has great significance. In regard to personal names, many cultures have naming ceremonies for their children, at which time it is believed the soul enters the body of the child. Almost every culture has traditions and rituals for the giving of names. Choosing, adopting, or changing one's name is sometimes part of a rite of passage. For example, most U.S. and European women, and increasing numbers of men, change their names upon marriage.

Because names connect us to our history, our families, and our culture, naming can be an act of dominance and a symbol of psychological and sometimes physical control of one person or group over another. (You may recall the scene in *Roots* when Kunta Kinte was forced to relinquish his African name and to become "Toby.") We frequently objectify individual humans by assigning them particular names or labels for their behavior or characteristics (e.g., *schizophrenic, blind, classy, girl*). By naming these ideas, we reify them.

Dominant groups, the groups in power, do not name themselves; they name other people. The others are named in relationship to the dominant group. When the first white explorers arrived in the territory called Alaska and asked the inhabitants what they called themselves, the people replied, "Eskimos," which means "people." Because the Eskimos were the only people around, they didn't need to name themselves in relationship to anyone else. The explorers, however, needed to distinguish the Eskimos as others, so they called them "Eskimos." In this book, we use names for the various racially defined ethnic groups that our clients have told us are preferred:

- African American
- Asian Pacific Islander
- European American
- Hispanic or Latino/Latina
- Native American Indian

For other cultural groups, we use the terms for which our client populations have stated a preference, including

- Differently abled or differently challenged
- Gay men
- Lesbians
- Men
- Older Americans
- Women

In a society where there are several ethnic cultures, one is usually dominant and consequently sets the norms for language and cultural expectations. The dominant culture has disproportionately greater political and economic power in a society. Professional, school, and social cultures are additional types of culture that affect the power relationships of people in a school environment. These types of cultures are important to recognize because people usually identify with several cultural groups. Therefore, each person in the school is represented by several types of cultures. It is from this amalgam of culture types that the dominant cultural patterns emerge within the school. As the school culture's dominant pattern emerges, it either embraces or marginalizes educators, parents, and students of nondominant cultural groups.

The culture of each organization—whether the organization is your family or your school—is what distinguishes it from other organizations. Each culture develops its own set of formal and informal processes to function. When you walk into a school building for the first time, you immediately get a sense of what type of school it is; whether it is a positive, healthy place for children; whether the administrator cares about what is going on; and whether someone will notice that you don't belong there. That feeling is your experience of the school's culture. You can go into several second grade classrooms, and each one will feel different; those distinctions reflect the culture of each classroom. Harrison (1992) calls this cultural milieu the school's "climate." The culturally proficient leader will understand that the overlay of school climate, student cultures, and professional cultures provides a unique mix that will affect each of the groups at the school in a different way. The culturally proficient leader ensures that cultures within the school are identified, articulated, and taught to increase understanding.

THE CULTURAL PROFICIENCY CONTINUUM

Cultural proficiency represents either the policies, practices, and procedures of a school or the values and behaviors of an individual that enable that school or person to interact effectively in a culturally diverse environment. Cultural proficiency is reflected in the way a school treats its faculty and staff, its students, and its surrounding community. The culturally proficient person does not claim to—or perhaps even attempt to—know everything there is to know about all cultural groups. Rather, a culturally proficient person knows how to learn about cultures and respond effectively to specific groups and situations.

Cultural proficiency is the optimum point on a continuum, the point at which educators and the school environment optimally facilitate effective cross-cultural interaction. Figure 2.2 presents the six points along the cultural proficiency continuum, which indicate unique ways of seeing and responding to difference.

Cultural Destructiveness	Cultural Blindness	Cultural Competence
Cultural Incapacity	Cultural Precompetence	Cultural Proficiency

Figure 2.2. The Cultural Proficiency Continuum

Culturally proficient educators recognize that *culture* involves far more than ethnic or racial differences. They demonstrate an understanding of the cacophony of diverse cultures each person experiences in the school setting. Although they accept that they will not necessarily have intimate knowledge about each of the cultures represented in a classroom, school, or district, they recognize their need to learn more continually. They develop a conscious awareness of the culture of their communities, districts, or schools, and they understand that each has a powerful effect on the educators, students, parents, and community associated with that school or district. As previously indicated, there are six points along the cultural proficiency continuum that indicate unique ways of seeing and responding to difference:

- **Cultural destructiveness:** The elimination of other people's cultures

- **Cultural incapacity:** Belief in the superiority of one's own culture and behavior that disempowers another's culture

- **Cultural blindness:** Acting as if the cultural differences one sees do not matter or not recognizing that there are differences among and between cultures

- **Cultural precompetence:** Awareness of the limitations of one's skills or an organization's practices when interacting with other cultural groups

- **Cultural competence:** Interacting with other cultural groups using the five essential elements of cultural proficiency as the standard for individual behavior and school practices: acceptance and respect for difference; ongoing assessment of one's own and the organization's culture; attention to the dynamics of difference; continuous expansion of cultural knowledge and resources; and the adaptation of one's values and behaviors and the organization's policies and practices

- **Cultural proficiency:** Esteeming culture; knowing how to learn about individual and organizational culture; interacting effectively in a variety of cultural environments

The continuum provides a perspective for examining policies, practices, and procedures in a school by giving reference points and a common language for describing historical or current situations. For instance, it is easy to apply the cultural proficiency continuum to events that have resulted in people being murdered, maimed, or exploited by dominant and destructive groups. More subtle outcomes, however, may be more difficult to categorize. Therefore, educators may need various opportunities to practice using the continuum to identify how students' opportunities have been preempted, denied, limited, or enhanced. As you read the following section, view the continuum using two trains of thought. First, read the material, adding your own illustrations showing how groups of people have been affected at various times in history. Second, use the continuum to examine how students have been—and are currently being—affected by practices in your school that either limit or enhance their opportunities.

The teachers at the Rolling Meadows Middle School have heard that the district is going to hire some consultants to teach them to be racially sensitive. They are neither impressed nor pleased. Sitting in the teachers' lunchroom, they speak wistfully about when their own children attended the district, failing to acknowledge that the demographics have been changing dramatically. Their comments range in attitude from culturally destructive to culturally proficient.

Cultural Destructiveness

"This is America, everyone should speak English."
"We didn't do anything to those people, why do we have to change?"
"This is America; they should be adapting to us."
"This is reverse discrimination."

The easiest to detect and the most negative end of the continuum is represented by attitudes, policies, and practices destructive to cultures and consequently to the individuals within a culture. Extreme examples include cultural genocide, such as the U.S. system of enslaving African captives and the North American westward expansion that resulted in the near-extinction of many Native American nations. Other examples of cultural destructiveness are the many Bureau of Indian Affairs educational programs that took young people from their families and tribes and placed them in boarding schools where the goal was to eradicate their language and culture. Additional examples include the mass exterminations of many peoples that have occurred in the 20th century. This century was witness to the Nazi extermination of Jews, gypsies, gay men, and lesbians, as well as others viewed as less than desirable by occupying forces. Other destructive acts have included the pogroms of Russia, the Turkish extermination of Armenians, and the killing fields of Southeast Asia, as well as the contemporary "ethnic cleansing" that has occurred in the Hutu-Tutsi wars of central Africa and in the former Yugoslav Republic.

Elementary and high schools historically have been places where students were socialized to become U.S. citizens and to learn basic skills for functioning in the workplace. In the 19th and early 20th century, this process of acculturation involved socializing people from all parts of Europe into an emerging dominant Anglo culture. This melting-pot approach to public school education was relatively effective within two to three generations for the European immigrants. Over the past 50 years, compulsory attendance requirements have brought into schools increasing numbers of Latinos, African Americans, Native Americans, immigrants from Southeast Asia, and indigenous European Americans from low socioeconomic groups. Although members of these groups have made striking successes in education, their acquisition of English proficiency and middle-class mores has not necessarily ensured their access either to higher education or to middle-class lifestyles. The cultural destructiveness that these groups have experienced in schools often results in markedly lower achievement, higher dropout rates, and lower social mobility. Specific examples of cultural destructiveness in schools include the following:

- Policies such as English only and the elimination of bilingual education programs so that children are essentially prohibited from using their native language at school
- Providing no acceptable options for girls who must not wear shorts or who must cover their heads at all times because their culture dictates a modest dress code

Cultural Incapacity

"I didn't know he is gay. He doesn't look gay to me."

"She catches well for a girl."

"I can't believe my Japanese boys only scored in the 80th percentile!"

The next point on the continuum describes an organization or individuals that show extreme bias, believe in the superiority of the dominant group, and assume a paternal posture toward so-called lesser groups. These systems or individuals are often characterized by ignorance, as well as either a dislike or an unrealistic fear of people who differ from the dominant group. Cultural incapacity virtually guarantees limited opportunities and can lead to *learned helplessness,* people's belief that they are powerless to help themselves because of their repeated experiences of powerlessness.

Historical examples include restrictive immigration laws targeting Asians and Pacific Islanders, such as the Oriental Exclusion Acts and the Jim Crow laws that denied African Americans basic human rights. Other examples include discriminatory hiring practices, generally lower expectations of performance for minority group members, and subtle messages to people who are not members of the dominant group conveying that they are not valued or welcomed. Specific examples of cultural incapacity in schools include

- Assuming that all African American families experience poverty
- Believing that it is inherently better to be heterosexual than homosexual
- Announcing that a new Latina has been hired to be a role model for Latinas, without recognizing that all children can profit from having role models from their own and other cultural groups

Cultural Blindness

"When I walk into a classroom, I do not see color or ability or gender, I only see children."

"Why are we trying to fix something that's not broken?"

The third point on the continuum, cultural blindness, is the most vexing point. Cultural blindness is the belief that color and culture make no difference and that all people are the same. For many educators, that is the goal of a diversity program. The values and behaviors of the dominant culture are presumed to be universally applicable and beneficial. The intention of the culturally blind educator is to avoid discriminating—that is, to avoid making an issue of the differences manifested among the students. Culturally blind educators too often view students' cultural differences to be indications of disobedience, noncompliance, or other deficiencies. They assume that members of minority cultures do not meet the cultural expectations of the dominant group because they lack either the cultural traditions of the dominant culture (i.e., they're culturally deficient) or the desire to achieve (i.e., they're morally deficient). In reality, the system works only for the most highly assimilated minority groups. As a result of many educators' blindness to the differences among students, too many students are left feeling discounted or invisible in school.

In our conversations with educators who prize their own cultural blindness, they are always painfully unaware of how their behavior affects their students. When confronted with the inappropriateness of cultural blindness, they initially retreat into the defensive position that they never intended to discriminate. It is difficult for good people who are committed to fairness to believe that they sometimes hurt their students. We explain in more detail in Chapter 3 that it is important not to focus on intentions but to become aware of the effect that educator behavior can have on students.

It is important for educators to recognize that students from nondominant groups view their differences as important aspects of their identity. Their differences also affect how they are viewed both within their respective communities and in the larger society. These educators are surprised to learn that black children would not choose to be anything other than black, that Cambodian children are proud of their language, and that the child in the wheelchair does not feel disadvantaged. Culturally proficient educators are aware of the importance of their students' cultures, the effect of students' experiences with cultural epithets, and the invisibility of many students in much of the school curricula.

Culturally blind educators may teach that Abraham Lincoln is a hero to all African Americans, assume that Cinco de Mayo is a Latin American holiday, and believe that girls are predisposed toward the arts rather than the sciences. Other examples of cultural blindness in schools include

- Leadership training that fails to address issues of diversity
- Lack of awareness that each school has its own unique culture and that each group experiences it differently
- Inability or failure to articulate the school's cultural expectations to all students, staff, and faculty members

Cultural Precompetence

"We need a Korean vice principal to help us with the Korean students."
"We celebrate Cinco de Mayo and Martin Luther King's birthday. What holiday can we use for Native American Indians?"
"Let's get some consultants in here to help us out."

Cultural precompetence is an awareness of limitations in cross-cultural communication and outreach. Although the culturally precompetent person wants to provide fair and equitable treatment with appropriate cultural sensitivity, this desire is accompanied by the frustration of not knowing exactly what is possible or how to proceed. An example is the belief that the accomplishment of a single goal or activity fulfills any perceived obligation toward minority groups; as a result, culturally precompetent educators may point with pride to the hiring of one disabled person or the serving of a soul food meal during Black History month as proof of a school's cultural proficiency. Other examples include

- Recruiting members of underrepresented groups but not providing support for them or making any adaptation to the differences they bring to the workplace
- Dismissing as overly sensitive anyone who complains about culturally inappropriate comments
- Failing to hold accountable any members of minority groups who are not performing well
- Making rules against hate speech instead of having a curriculum that teaches the cherishing of history, cultures, and languages that are different

Cultural Competence

"To really understand student needs, we must disaggregate these test data."

"Let's look at the school calendar to make sure we don't schedule our potlucks during Ramadan, Ridvan, or Yom Kippur."[2]

At the point of cultural competence, schools and educators accept and respect differences, carefully attend to the dynamics of difference, continually assess their own cultural knowledge and beliefs, continuously expand their cultural knowledge and resources, and make various adaptations of their own belief systems, policies, and practices. This is the first point on the continuum that fully addresses the needs of diverse student populations. Culturally competent educators

- Incorporate culturally appropriate behavior in performance appraisals
- Model culturally inclusive behaviors (e.g., learning to speak Spanish in a predominantly Latino community)
- Speak on issues about handicapped persons, gay men, and lesbians when no representatives of these groups are visibly present
- Advocate for changes in policies, practices, and procedures throughout the school and community
- Teach communication strategies that lead to understanding of other people's views
- Teach cultural variables in conflict resolution

Cultural Proficiency

"I believe that conflict is natural and normal; I'm glad we are learning how to do things differently when conflict occurs."

"Our goal for examining our school policy on student grouping must be to enhance student achievement."

Cultural proficiency is more than the esteeming of culture. A culturally competent educator functions effectively in several different cultural contexts. The culturally proficient educator knows how to learn about culture. Confronted with the challenges of a new cultural setting, culturally proficient educators know how to find out what they need to know in a nonoffensive manner. The culturally proficient leader seeks to add to the knowledge base of culturally proficient practices by conducting research, developing new approaches based on culture, taking every available opportunity to increase formally and informally the awareness level and knowledge base of others about culture and about the dynamics of difference. Culturally proficient leaders do the following:

- Unabashedly advocate for culturally proficient practices in all arenas
- Help develop curriculum based on what is known about multiple intelligences
- Take advantage of teachable moments to learn of and teach their colleagues about culturally proficient practices

WHAT IS CULTURALLY PROFICIENT BEHAVIOR?

The cultural proficiency continuum takes a broad look at the range of behaviors and attitudes that address the issues of diversity. This section describes the specific behaviors that must be present within your school and yourself as an educator for you to be culturally proficient. We call these behaviors the five essential elements of cultural proficiency: (1) value diversity, (2) assess one's own culture, (3) manage the dynamics of difference, (4) institutionalize cultural knowledge, and (5) adapt to diversity. Figure 2.3 provides examples of the essential elements.

Value Diversity

As a culturally proficient leader, you are proactive in involving a wide variety of people from all areas of the school. You demonstrate your valuing of diversity by openly addressing the need to serve all persons who are different effectively, and you accept that cultures vary, evoking different feelings and behaviors. As a culturally proficient school leader, you provide leadership in developing policy statements on diversity or ensuring that the school and district's mission and goal statements include the concept of diversity. You take these statements and act on them by communicating inclusion to marginalized groups and by directing human and financial resources into curricular, training, and other school endeavors to address diversity proactively.

1. **Value Diversity** (Name the Differences)
   - Celebrate and encourage the presence of a variety of people in all activities
   - Recognize difference as diversity rather than as inappropriate responses to the environment
   - Accept that each culture finds some values and behaviors more important than others

2. **Assess One's Culture** (Claim Your Identity)
   - Describe your own culture and the cultural norms of your organization
   - Recognize how your culture affects others
   - Understand how the culture of your organization affects those whose culture is different

3. **Manage the Dynamics of Difference** (Frame the Conflicts)
   - Learn effective strategies for resolving conflict among people whose cultural backgrounds and values may be different from yours
   - Understand the effect that historic distrust has on present day interactions
   - Realize that you may misjudge others' actions based on learned expectations

4. **Institutionalize Cultural Knowledge** (Train About Diversity)
   - Integrate into your systems for staff development and education, information and skills that enable all to interact effectively in a variety of cross-cultural situations
   - Incorporate cultural knowledge into the mainstream of the organization
   - Teach origins of stereotypes and prejudices

5. **Adapt to Diversity** (Change for Diversity)
   - Change the way things are done to acknowledge the differences that are present in the staff, patients, and community
   - Develop skills for cross-cultural communication
   - Institutionalize cultural interventions for conflicts and confusion caused by the dynamics of difference

Figure 2.3. The Essential Elements of Cultural Proficiency

As a culturally proficient school leader, you celebrate and encourage a value for diversity in all activities by

- Ensuring that all stakeholders in the school community are involved in the process
- Recognizing difference as diversity rather than as inappropriate responses to the school setting
- Accepting that each culture finds some values and behaviors more important than others

Assess Your Culture

To assess your culture, you analyze yourself and your environment so that you have a palpable sense of your own culture and the culture of your school. The purpose of assessing your culture directly relates to the inside-out approach of the cultural proficiency model. As a culturally proficient educator, you start with yourself and your own school. You do not assume that everyone will share your values, nor do you assume that everyone knows what behaviors are expected and affirmed in a culturally proficient school; in fact, most persons are simply unaware. Therefore, you understand how the culture of your school and district affects those whose culture is different. You will state and explain the cultural norms of each classroom, school, or district so that people whose cultural norms differ from those will know how they must adapt to the new environment. By recognizing how the school's culture affects other people, you will gain the data you need to make adjustments in style or processes so that all people feel comfortable and welcomed. As a culturally proficient leader, you

- Understand how the culture of your school affects those whose culture is different
- Describe your own culture and the cultural norms of your school
- Recognize how your school's culture affects others

Manage the Dynamics of Difference

A school that values diversity is not without conflict. As a culturally proficient leader, you acknowledge that conflict is a natural state of affairs and you develop effective, culturally proficient strategies for managing the conflict that occurs. Once you have embraced the value for diversity and have begun to articulate the cultural expectations of your school or classroom, the differences among the school's community members will be more apparent. You will be ready for this situation by providing an opportunity for everyone in the school community to learn effective strategies for resolving conflict among people whose backgrounds differ. As a leader, you will provide training sessions and facilitate group discussions so that people will understand the effect of historical distrust on present-day interactions. You realize that the actions of others may be misjudged based on learned expectations, and you implement programs and processes that create new cultural expectations for the culturally proficient community. As a culturally proficient leader, you

- Learn effective strategies for resolving conflict among people whose cultural backgrounds and values may differ from yours

- Understand how historical distrust affects present-day interactions

- Realize that you may misjudge other people's actions based on learned expectations

Institutionalize Cultural Knowledge

As a culturally proficient school leader, you prize ongoing staff development that promotes a commitment to lifelong learning. You clearly understand that information and technology are evolving at an ever-quickening pace, thereby dictating the need for continuous upgrading of knowledge and skills. Similarly, as our society continues increasingly to appreciate its multicultural nature and its intimate interconnections with the wider world, you recognize the increasing importance of cultural proficiency. You readily integrate into systems of staff development and education the information and skills that enable educators and students to interact effectively in a variety of cross-cultural situations. You affirm the importance of cultural knowledge, not only for the climate of the school or district but also as a knowledge base on which all students will continue to build throughout their lives.

As a culturally proficient leader, you also realize that students need knowledge about both the cultural practices of different people and groups and the experiences that many of these people and groups have had with stereotyping and prejudice. With this awareness, you provide your school communities with an understanding of how prejudices and stereotypes are developed and maintained in the society. You also help students and colleagues develop skills for eliminating prejudices through various human interactions, curricula, and instructional programs in schools. As a culturally proficient leader, you

- Integrate into the educational system the information and skills needed for effective interaction in a variety of cross-cultural situations
- Incorporate cultural knowledge into the mainstream of the school
- Take advantage of evolving classroom interactions that arise related to issues of differences, and use those teachable moments and other opportunities to learn from or to teach to one another

Adapt to Diversity

To adapt to diversity is first to recognize that everyone changes. In traditional approaches to diversity, such as throwing everyone into the melting pot, the groups that are not a part of the dominant culture are expected to change and to adapt to the culture of the dominant group. The culturally proficient approach to diversity invites and encourages everyone to change. Once you make the commitment to cultural proficiency, you help all aspects of the school community to adapt. You help the host groups change by becoming more conscious of cultural norms that deny the value of diversity and the goal of cultural proficiency. You encourage the newer or less dominant groups to change because they know clearly the cultural expectations of the school. You enable the school or district to change by using culturally proficient behaviors as the standards for performance appraisal and as the basis for analyzing and revising school and district policies. As a culturally proficient leader, you

- Change the way things are done by acknowledging the differences that are present in the faculty, staff, students, and community

- Examine policies and practices that may convey benign discrimination
- Institutionalize cultural interventions that address the conflict and confusion caused by the dynamics of difference

GUIDING PRINCIPLES OF CULTURAL PROFICIENCY

By taking deliberately and systematically implementing the behavior outlined in the preceding five essential elements of cultural proficiency, you can achieve cultural proficiency for yourself and your school. To carry out this ambitious task, you need a firm value base. With such a base, you can transform a daunting challenge into an opportunity that brings all people together to create a culturally proficient district or school. The cultural proficiency model includes five principles, presented in Figure 2.4, that may help to guide you as you work toward cultural proficiency. This section describes the guiding principles and comments we have heard while working in various schools and school districts.

On the other side of the county, Coolidge Unified District serves the families that live in the urban center where many Rolling Meadows adults work. The district is working with Jim Woodard, a diversity consultant. At the first staff development session, Jim explains the underlying principles that inform his approach to dealing with diversity. He hears some interesting comments as the teachers and administrators leave the session for the afternoon.

Culture Is Ever Present

"I don't have a culture. I'm just a generic person. Heinz 57."
"Doesn't focusing on differences just make it harder for us to get along?"

Your culture is a defining aspect of your humanity. It is the predominant force in shaping values and behaviors. Occasionally, you may be inclined to take offense at behaviors that differ from yours, but as a culturally proficient leader, remind yourself that offensive behavior may not be personal; it may be cultural. Recognize that members of so-called minority populations have to be at least bicultural, and this creates its own set of issues, problems, and possible conflicts. All people who are not a part of

- **Culture Is Ever Present**

  Acknowledge culture as a predominant force in shaping behaviors, values, and institutions. Although you may be inclined to take offense at the behaviors that differ from yours, remind yourself that it may not be personal; it may be cultural.

- **People Are Served in Varying Degrees by the Dominant Culture**

  What works well in organizations and in the community for you, and others who are like you, may work against members of other cultural groups. Failure to make such an acknowledgment puts the burden for change on one group.

- **People Have Group Identities and Personal Identities**

  Although it is important to treat all people as individuals, it is also important to acknowledge the group identity of individuals. Actions must be taken with the awareness that the dignity of a person is not guaranteed unless the dignity of his or her people is also preserved.

- **Diversity Within Cultures Is Important**

  Because diversity within cultures is as important as diversity between cultures, it is important to learn about cultural groups not as monoliths (e.g., Asians, Hispanics, gay men, and women) but as the complex and diverse groups that they are. Often, because of the class differences in the United States, there will be more in common across cultural lines than within them.

- **Each Group Has Unique Cultural Needs**

  Each cultural group has unique needs that cannot be met within the boundaries of the dominant culture. Expressions of one group's cultural identity do not imply a disrespect for yours. Make room in your organization for several paths that lead to the same goal.

Figure 2.4. The Guiding Principles of Cultural Proficiency

the dominant group have already gained competence in one culture before they began to learn standard English or dominant U.S. cultural norms. Therefore, when members of nondominant cultures resist or hesitate in using the language or cultural norms of the dominant culture, they are not necessarily ignorant or incompetent; rather, they simply may be using language or cultural behaviors with which they are more familiar or more comfortable.

Culturally proficient educators recognize that what they experience as normal or regular is part of their culture. This may tempt them to feel a sense of entitlement, but by recognizing these feelings, they can then acknowledge and appreciate the subtle cultural differences among members of the dominant culture. Rarely do today's European Americans experience the process of acquiring another language or a new set of values, norms, or behaviors. They also less seldom need to seek appropriate and accepted places for using their first language and culture. This lack of experience often leads to misunderstanding and a lack of awareness of what it means to be perceived as different on a day-by-day basis. It also insulates members of the dominant culture from the negative judgments ascribed to people because of their linguistic and cultural differences. As we come to understand the reality of exclusion experienced by members of minority groups, it becomes possible to turn such understanding into a value for diversity.

People Are Served in Varying Degrees by the Dominant Culture

"I don't see why they can't adjust like the rest of us did."
"All of us have suffered discrimination."

Culturally proficient educators adjust their behaviors and values to accommodate the full range of diversity represented by their school populations. They recognize that some individuals from minority cultures find success in varying degrees in schools where only the dominant culture is acknowledged and valued. Although educators and students in the dominant culture may profit from such a setting, and some members of some nondominant groups may do well despite such a setting, many other students and educators may find such an atmosphere stifling and limiting. Such an imbalance of power puts the total burden for change on one person or group. Culturally proficient leaders see the need to ensure that members of dominant groups, historically oppressed groups, and new cultural groups share the responsibility for change.

People Have Group Identities
and Personal Identities

"You sure didn't sound black on the phone when we talked."
"I didn't know there were Chinese people over 6 feet tall."

It is important to treat all people as individuals as well as to acknowledge each group's identity. It demeans and insults individuals and their cultures to single out particular assimilated members of ethnic groups and to tell them that they differ from members of their own group, implying that their differentness somehow makes them better, or more acceptable, to the dominant group. Culturally proficient leaders know that to guarantee the dignity of each person, they must also preserve the dignity of each person's culture.

Often, so-called personality problems are actually problems of cultural differences. Culturally proficient leaders address these problems. They recognize that cultural differences in thought patterns (e.g., those of non-Western, non-European people vs. those of Westerners) reflect differing but equally valid ways of viewing and solving problems. No cultural group appears exclusively to use just one particular approach for processing information and solving problems, although some cultures are traditionally associated with one approach more than others. Nor is there evidence that one approach is superior to others across all situations. Culturally proficient leaders recognize these and other cultural differences, and they use this knowledge to promote effective communication among diverse people.

Diversity Within Cultures Is Important

"You are different, we're very comfortable with you."
"We would have more of your kind around if they were just like you."

Because diversity within cultures is as important as diversity between cultures, it is important to learn about ethnic groups not as monoliths (e.g., Asians, Latinos, or whites) but as the complex and diverse groups that they are. Within each major ethnic group are many distinctive subgroups. Often, because of the class differences in the United States, there will be more in common across ethnic lines than within them. For example, upper-middle-class U.S. citizens of European, African, and Japanese descent will be more likely to share values and a similar worldview than will members of any one ethnic group who come from varying socioeconomic backgrounds, from working class to upper class. Culturally proficient schools recognize these intracultural differences and provide their faculty, staff, students, and parents with access to information about people who are not like themselves in various ways. These schools create an environment that fosters trust, safety, and the enhancement of self for the people who work and learn in them.

Each Group Has Unique Cultural Needs

"Why do they have to have a special program?"

"I think everyone should be given the same attention and information. That's fair."

European Americans can assume that a public school in this country will have information about the history and culture of their people in the United States, as well as about their countries of origin. Other U.S. citizens and U.S. immigrants cannot make such assumptions. The culturally proficient educator will teach and encourage colleagues who are members of the dominant culture to make the necessary adaptations in how schools provide educational service so that all people have access to the same benefits and privileges as members of the dominant group in society.

One of the barriers to cultural proficiency is a lack of awareness of the need to adapt. The first step toward removing that barrier is to recognize that highlighting the best aspects of all people represented in the community enhances the capacity of everyone. If educators in a school try to develop their cultural proficiency by increasing the value for diversity, assessing the school's culture, and institutionalizing cultural knowledge, then they will increase people's awareness of the need to adapt, as well as people's respect for the unique cultural needs of diverse populations.

NOTES

1. We recognize that the term *American* is more common than *U.S. citizens*. We choose to use *U.S.* when speaking of the United States of America or its citizens because it is more specific and it acknowledges that there are Americans on two continents, not just in one country.

2. These are the holidays of the Muslim, Baha'i and Jewish faiths, respectively, that require the faithful to fast during the day. Ramadan and Ridvan last for several weeks, so your Muslim and Baha'i colleagues and students may be at school while fasting.

THREE

Becoming a Culturally Proficient Leader

The opinions of the faculty and administration at Rolling Meadows reflect the range of views in the community. Many believe that the school can be organized to provide a quality education for all students. A smaller and very vocal group continually decries any changes that appear to lower standards and accuses the administration of the school and district of not supporting the school by getting tough with troublemakers. Members of this group believe that if the school returns to a well-defined tracking system that creates a vocational level for students who are not interested in learning, then the needs of everyone will be served. They also believe that senior teachers should be given first choice for teaching courses.

This vocal minority among the veteran faculty continues to protest loudly the many changes occurring at the school. The faculty who have been at the school for fewer than 10 years tend to be much more culturally diverse. The principal is African American, and her administrative staff comprises a white male vice principal and two assistant principals who are a white female and a Latina. The white male has been an administrator at the school for 12 years, and the principal and assistant principals have been at the school 3 years or less. The principal and assistant principals are often perceived as affirmative action placements.

CULTURALLY PROFICIENT SCHOOL LEADERS

When asked about school leadership, most people in the school community focus on various specific behaviors they observe in formal leaders, then judge how those behaviors measure up against what they believe to be appropriate behaviors. Some people prefer leaders who leave them alone, whereas others prefer leaders who are deeply involved with them in their classrooms. Everyone has a different list of specific items. In this book, we prefer to broaden our vision, to look at the overall qualities of leadership, particularly qualities that facilitate movement toward cultural proficiency. In this chapter, we provide a context for understanding the leadership at your school, a necessary step for developing culturally proficient leadership skills in yourself and in those with whom you work. This discussion includes the following topics:

- How should we define leadership and its practice?
- What do culturally proficient educational leaders do?
- Who are the formal and nonformal leaders in your schools?
- What is the historical context for the kind of educational leadership that exists today?

Leadership can be positive, motivating others to excel and to move in desirable directions, or negative, serving to diffuse or otherwise block plans for change. In either case, contemporary researchers have found that effective leaders consistently show several key characteristics (Argyris, 1990; Banks, 1994; Senge et al., 1994; Wheatley, 1992) wherever that leadership occurs (from private businesses to corporate enterprise to local school districts). These ingredients include taking responsibility for one's own learning, having a vision for what the school can be, effectively sharing the vision with others, assessing one's own assumptions and beliefs, and understanding the structural and organic nature of schools. We have observed that culturally proficient leaders show these characteristics, whether they do so intuitively or as a result of carefully studying how to lead effectively. Further, culturally proficient leaders learn about themselves, those with whom they work, and the school within which they work. Their study of themselves and their schools is fundamental to cultural proficiency, our inside-out approach to addressing issues of diversity introduced in Chapter 2.

The formal leadership of schools has historically been the domain of white men. Although trends of change are emerging, the demographic profile of formal school leaders remains predominantly white and male. Educational data (National Center for Educational Statistics, 1994) show that 84% of district administrators and 77% of principals and assistant principals are white, and 59% of district administrators and 60% of assistant principals and principals are male. Perhaps because white men are mainly in charge of the development of school systems, many of the educational policies and practices have tended to benefit members of the dominant culture more than other people. For instance, in their attempts to apply rules of science to school leadership, educators have developed top-down organization structures, systems for tracking students of differing abilities, and standardized tests to ensure that students are learning.

We have found that educators often have differing definitions of leadership. The definition we provide here, based on our own experiences in educational leadership, has proven useful in our work with educational leaders. Whereas school administration is the process of getting work done through others, *leadership* is the process of inspiring others to work together to achieve a specific goal. Nowadays, virtually any book you pick up on school leadership emphasizes the importance of leaders having and communicating a vision, guiding the creation of a shared mission, and building strong school cultures (Gilligan, 1983; Oakes & Lipton, 1990; Ogbu, 1978; Sizer, 1985). Effective leaders have four things:

1. A vision of what the group can be that is greater than what it is
2. The ability to communicate that vision in language that is understood by the prospective followers
3. The skills to assess and respond appropriately to the needs of the people and the environment in which they are working
4. The values and personality needed to build a strong school culture (Argryis, 1990; Fullan, 1991; Owens, 1991; Wheatley, 1992)

Usually, when we speak of leaders, we think of formal leaders, those who have titles and official positions according them a certain degree of authority and coercive power. Although nonformal leaders have no official role assigning them the authority to direct a group, they have personal attributes—such as charisma, vision, and eloquence—that cause people to listen and to take action. A nonformal leader can be more powerful than a formal leader because the attributes of leadership are internally driven rather than externally conferred.

THE CULTURALLY PROFICIENT SCHOOL LEADER

Massey (1979a) asserts that each of us is a product of the decades in which we were born and raised and that the values inherent in those time periods do as much to shape our perspectives as anything else does. This assertion seems to hold true for many educational practices. Educators too often accept roles as teachers, administrators, counselors, or other school-related professionals without assessing many of the practices in the school, let alone understanding how these practices came into use.

In analyzing current practices, leaders must be able to identify issues of class, caste, culture, and gender. Ogbu's (1978) notion of a caste system in this country yields a crucial observation about poverty and racism: It is no accident that low-achieving students in this country are overrepresented by African American, Latino, and Native American students who are from families of lower socioeconomic status. In this country, the apparent permanence of these socioeconomic groups gives rise to the reality of caste systems not unlike those many people assume exist in other countries.

Similarly, Freire's (1970) view of the poor teaching provided to the lowest economic groups of this nation provides a stark view of the role of schools. His work with people around the world, most notably in Latin American countries, has illustrated time and again that students and their families are capable of high levels of achievement if they are taught how to learn, provided with the resources to learn, and given a reason to believe that they can control their own destinies. Gilligan's (1983) work on gender issues illustrates how the male-centered perspective in this country has too often denied women the educational and other advantages afforded to half of the population.

The teaching of Ogbu (1978), Freire (1970), and Gilligan (1983) correlates with cultural proficiency theory. Culturally proficient leaders are guided by theory in developing first a vision and then a mission that serves the needs of all students. In addition, they recognize the formal and nonformal systems in the school, know about the cultural issues that affect learning, and have access to the resources necessary for an appropriate learning environment within the school. Culturally proficient school leaders know and appreciate how different school systems have evolved and are equipped to work with people and to guide others in challenging their own assumptions and translating their perspectives, perceptions, values, and goals into agendas for school change. Having this knowledge of systems enables them to assess the formal and nonformal leadership structures of their schools. They are able to support and lead school personnel as they formulate their plan for school change.

ANALYZING SCHOOL LEADERSHIP

As a culturally proficient school leader, you need to understand what currently exists before you can begin to understand what *should* exist (Giroux, 1992). Table 3.1 provides a matrix by which to examine schools. The columns list the most typical roles of school leaders (school district administrators, site administrators, teachers, parents and other community members, and school board members) and identify the function that role plays in creating a culturally proficient school or district. The rows represent the five essential elements of cultural proficiency outlined in Chapter 2 (value diversity, assess culture, manage the dynamics of difference, institutionalize cultural knowledge, and adapt to diversity) and describe behaviors related to each of the elements. In constructing this table and the discussion that follows, we have drawn on the works of Argyris (1990), Banks (1994), Senge et al. (1994), and Wheatley (1992). Their combined works affirm our inside-out approach to culturally proficient leadership. Together, they provide two frameworks: (1) an *inwardly oriented framework* for examining assumptions about those who culturally differ from ourselves, for understanding how our schools function, and

TABLE 3.1 Responsibilities of Culturally Proficient School Leaders

ROLES

Elements of Cultural Proficiency	Teachers *Observe and Instruct*	Site Administrators *Lead and Supervise*	District Administrators *Implement Policy*	Parents and Community *Articulate Expectations*	School Board Members *Set Policy*
Value Diversity	Teach all subjects from a culturally inclusive perspective	Articulate a culturally proficient vision for the site	Provide guidelines for culturally proficient practices and establish standards for appraisal	Elect school board members who represent the diversity of the community	Define and establish criteria for culturally proficient practices
Assess Culture	Assess own culture and its effect on students; assess the culture of the classroom; support students in discovering their own cultural identity	Assess culture of the site	Assess culture of the district and the administrator's role in maintaining or changing it	Share with school personnel the community members' perceptions of the schools' cultures	Assess the culture of the district; assess the culture of the board and the effect of that culture on the community it serves
Manage the Dynamics of Difference	Use conflict as a tool for object lessons; teach students a variety of ways to resolve conflict	Provide training and support systems for conflict resolution	Provide resources for developing and establishing new conflict resolution strategies	Discern the nature and source of conflict when it occurs (i.e., racism, sexism, etc.)	Articulate the need and value for conflict resolution in the context of diversity
Institutionalize Cultural Knowledge	Teach students appropriate language for asking questions about other people's cultures and telling other people about theirs	Model and monitor schoolwide and classroom practices	Propose and carry out all policies from a cultural proficiency perspective	Serve as resources and reference groups	Establish all policies from a culturally proficient perspective
Adapt to Diversity	Learn own instructional and interpersonal strengths and weaknesses; develop processes to compensate for them	Assess and change current practices where appropriate	Assess policy and propose changes where appropriate	Identify policies and practices that need changing	Review and change policies to maintain cultural proficiency as the student population changes

54

for seeing how each school's culture facilitates learning for some students and impedes others from learning; and (2) an *outwardly directed framework* for discovering how and why we learn about others, engage in team learning, and examine data for the purpose of making informed changes in school practices.

In culturally proficient schools, each participant has a definite role to play. The roles overlap in some instances, but they retain distinctive characteristics. Clearly, some people will be more proficient at executing their distinctive roles than will others. Barriers to culturally proficient leadership arise from myriad sources. For instance, in school districts that have traditionally failed to involve parents and community members in school decision-making processes, part of the movement toward cultural proficiency will be to help parents and community members learn their roles. Some of them will be reticent to be involved, whereas others may manifest anger at being excluded for so long. Still other parents and community members will clearly articulate their expectations of what they want the school to do for their children. As a culturally proficient leader, you recognize that silence does not mean a lack of interest or concern, just as anger does not signify parents' irreverence for their children's educators. You will have to develop processes to involve these diverse people in school matters. In addition to responding to these differences, you must remain committed to listening for the messages of wanting to be involved and then providing support for involvement.

BARRIERS TO CULTURAL PROFICIENCY

In other school districts, role conflicts may pose barriers to cultural proficiency. For instance, the recent history between teachers and district administrators may have been so acrimonious that civility appears to be rare. In this situation, too, the culturally proficient leader must listen for messages of wanting to be involved. Leaders in various roles implement cultural proficiency in divergent ways:

- Community leaders and parents communicate to educators what they want their children to gain from their education.

- School board members set school policy that represents the wishes of the community in serving the diverse needs of their children. They work with school leaders to determine policies that ensure the application of the essential elements of cultural proficiency.

- District-level administrators implement the policies of the board of education, acting as a conduit between the school board and the local schools. Not only do they interpret policy with those at the local schools, but they also carry data about local schools back to the district office to inform decision making about future changes in policies or procedures.

- Site administrators have the responsibility to provide formal leadership at the local school and to supervise for the purpose of providing support to classroom teachers.

Classrooms are where the action is, and classroom teachers have the responsibility to carry out curricular and instructional programs consistent with the district's cultural proficiency policies. They also have the responsibility to observe their students, to raise questions about student needs, and to work with site administrators in gathering data about student achievement and social interactions for the purpose of continuing to improve the educational climate at the school.

FORMAL LEADERSHIP AND BEYOND

The formal leadership of schools has historically been the domain of white men. Although trends of change are emerging, the demographic profile of formal school leaders remains predominantly white and male. Schools and districts where members of historically underrepresented groups have assumed formal leadership positions are often no more culturally responsive than those run by members of the dominant group. When looking at the national profile of school leaders and the universities that educate and train them, we see primarily a fraternity of European Americans. We must therefore remember that even if we change the faces of leaders but not the policies and practices that influence student achievement, the students may not fare any better. Perhaps because white men are mainly in charge of the development of school systems, many of the educational policies and practices have tended to benefit members of the dominant culture more than other people. For instance, in their attempts to apply rules of science to school leadership, educators have developed top-down organization structures, systems for tracking students of differing abilities, and standardized tests to ensure that students are learning.

Collegial Leadership

Most studies of—and approaches to—educational leadership focus on the formal leadership domain, neglecting the nonformal leaders in schools. Of course, the people who work with and in schools recognize the vital importance of nonformal leaders. Successful superintendents and principals are adept at multiplying their efforts through working with teachers, staff members, students, parents, and other community members who are respected by their constituents. In this chapter, we focus mainly on formal leaders, secondarily addressing the key role of nonformal leaders in school. We do so because we believe that formal leaders should bear the primary burden of responsibility for creating the changes described in this book. The formal leaders of schools— namely, the superintendents, district office administrators, site-level administrators, and teachers—are employed to educate all children. How well they use the skills of the nonformal leaders such as students, parents, community members, and key staff members measures their success.

Within the formal system, school leaders are primarily selected or elected via official public processes. Typically, vacancies are announced to the public, applications are submitted, interviews take place, selections are made, and appointments are announced. These positions usually include assistant principals, principals, and teacher organization and union representatives. When educators, students, and members of the community talk about leadership, they are usually talking about the formal leaders, such as the principal of the local school, the superintendent of the district, or one of the other people who has an out-of-classroom assignment.

Leatha Harp, director of credentialing and certification in Coolidge School District, has gathered a small team of teachers and administrators who have agreed to serve on employment interview panels this school year to hire administrators for the district. The team is reviewing anonymous comments written by other teachers and administrators when asked to discuss the type of leaders desired at Coolidge schools. The team has pulled out the comment sheets that reflect trends or themes in the responses. About the formal leaders in the district, team members read:

- What that school needs is a strict disciplinarian so the kids will know who is in charge.
- The Latino kids need a Latino administrator so they can have a positive role model.
- Principals come and go, but I will always be here.
- This school is entirely too tough for a woman administrator!
- I may not agree with her, but I know where she stands.
- One thing I will have to give the principal, he sure does relate well to the parents.
- She may be an expert in instruction and supervision, but how can she evaluate my physics lesson?

"I had no idea the comments would be so personal," exclaims Brittney, one of the middle school teachers. "They sound so jaded."

"Oh, they are not all bad," says Leatha. "They tell us a lot about what people want in their leaders."

"Look at this pile of comments," Leatha continues. "They tell us a lot about where the nonformal leadership is in this district."

"What do you mean by nonformal?" asks Grace. The ink is still wet on her credential.

"Nonformal leaders are not officially appointed or chosen, but rather emerge spontaneously, based on the needs and aspirations of those who work in the school environment," explains Leatha.

"Nonformal leaders usually mean people like teachers, aides, students, or parents. People who don't have official titles, but who have a lot of influence. Grace Ishmael, the director of the Citizens Human Relations Council, is a nonformal leader. She doesn't have such a high position, but everyone respects her and listens when she speaks. She is always at the district offices and the board meetings. Look at these comments; they acknowledge the nonformal leadership we have in this district."

- That secretary has trained seven principals!
- As a new teacher, it is best to get on the good side of the secretary and the lead custodian.

- If you want to reach out to the parents, just tell Mr. Nguyen, Kim's father—he is well respected in this community.

- To include more bilingual parents in school governance, you may want to use the services of the aide in Room 7; she has the ability to reach out well.

- The union representative is a very important member of the leadership council, but Mrs. Sandoval is the teacher to whom the others look for guidance.

- Why do the Athletic Boosters wield so much power?

Leaders, then, come from all sectors of the school and the community it serves. One crucial source of leadership is students. In our experience, student leadership is vital to culturally proficient leadership in schools. Schools exist for students to gain knowledge and skills for adult life. In the United States and the international community of today and tomorrow, these skills and knowledge include the ability to work in multicultural environments. Despite student leaders' importance, however, we focus herein almost entirely on the roles of adults in the school and community. Why? Because we believe that students should not have to bear the responsibility to lead change, although effective leaders will find ways for them to contribute their influence. Effective leaders acknowledge and support student leaders while assuming their own primary responsibility for making the school work for all students. Ideally, they do so proactively, with foresight and vision, rather than reactively, responding to student or community pressures with the gift of hindsight.

Changing Styles of Leadership

The definition of school leadership has begun to change rapidly, as have the specific responsibilities of school administrators. Contemporary school leaders are increasingly expected to nurture leadership by recognizing and valuing the skills of both formal and nonformal leaders. This expectation represents a paradigm shift for those educated and trained in traditional ways and those who work in traditionally organized schools. They are being pressured to change by union advocacy, community members' dissatisfaction with low student attendance and performance, and teachers' demands to be involved in decision making.

The evolving nature of leadership in U.S. schools involves teacher leadership through union activities and the expansion of the roles of parents and community members. The roles and responsibilities of school administrators, particularly site-level administrators, are undergoing rapid transformation to more participative practices. These participative practices are consistent with the observations that (1) relationships are fundamental to moving schools forward (Wheatley, 1992), and (2) shared vision and team learning are fundamental to developing schools for learning (Senge et al., 1994). Culturally proficient leaders prize these participative practices as a normal part of how they organize their work in the school. Culturally proficient leaders see their schools as learning organizations devoted to self-study, as well as to learning about the community and its children. Owens (1991) summarizes the newly emerging role of educational leaders:

> This has heightened our awareness that the power of educational leaders emanates not so much from their legal clout as from their ability to elicit the enthusiastic voluntary involvement of others—including students, teachers, community residents, and those in the official hierarchy—in the never-ending processes of creating and perfecting the educational institution. (p. ix)

Culturally proficient principals exercise leadership by using the talents of other leaders in the school community. They fully appreciate and know how to involve widely diverse constituencies in making their school work for children.

CHOOSING EFFECTIVE LEADERS

In most areas of the country, any impetus for placing people of color and women into formal leadership positions has been preceded by actual or pending legislation or by precedent-setting court cases. Nonetheless, gender and race still correlate very highly with who gains formal leadership roles in schools. Culturally proficient school leaders recognize that schools profit from having multiple perspectives, including those based on differences in gender, ethnicity, social class, sexual orientation, or physical or sensory ability. To this end, when filling formal and nonformal leadership positions, culturally proficient leaders actively solicit people who represent the widest spectrum of views.

Once a diverse group of leaders is in formal leadership roles, the leaders must be coached and supported in their new roles. They need support systems to be able to develop successful leadership behaviors further. In the past, the support system for white males was often referred to as the "good old boys' club." Although that infrastructure still exists in many school districts, in culturally proficient school districts, it is being replaced by formal systems of mentoring, in which all new administrators are formally inducted into their leadership positions. States such as California have gone so far as to formalize approaches to mentoring through the state administrator certification process (California Commission on Teacher Credentialing, 1995). Likewise, organizations of professional administrators have embraced notions of mentoring and coaching as part of their responsibility for seeing to the success of new administrators.

THE PROCESS OF LEADERSHIP

The information in these next sections, and its application to schools, gives culturally proficient school leaders a framework within which they can understand their own school. From this base of information, you can guide others in creating a shared vision of education for students at your school and in analyzing current practices to modify these appropriately, thereby facilitating student achievement.

A school cannot become culturally proficient without effective leadership. Someone or some group has to have a vision of a culturally proficient school or district. Someone has to communicate that vision to the administrators, teachers, and community members and inspire them to transform themselves.

Rolling Meadows Superintendent Watson recognizes that the demographics of the district are beginning to shift from being almost totally white to increasingly multicultural. He has gathered data on student achievement, openly noted the race-related fights at the high schools, and heard parents' complaints about the curriculum.

The RFP (request for proposal) that his staff prepares seeks consultants to conduct a year-long cultural audit and needs assessment that taps into the views and beliefs of all sectors of the district—the educators, the staff, the students, and members of the community. Although he has not yet been introduced to the concept of cultural proficiency, the superintendent knows intuitively to move in this comprehensive direction and to involve many layers of the district administration for them to understand his vision for all students in the district. He uses his formal position to lead the district into this diversity needs assessment process.

Watson, the formal leader, has a vision for maintaining the school district's excellence during a time of changing student population. Instead of accepting declining test scores, initiating repressive discipline measures at the high schools, or turning a deaf ear to parents, he gathers data so that the district can examine its practices and make necessary changes based on the data and consistent with the district's values. Argyris (1990) refers to this process as *double-loop learning,* in which school leaders gather data to determine leverage points where changes in the school system are needed. In this case, the leverage points are student achievement, teachers' perceptions of a need for higher expectations, interracial clashes among students, and parental complaints about curriculum. Rather than blaming the teachers, the students, the students' families, or their cultural experiences for these areas of weakness, Watson gathers information to improve the school's processes. In the case of student achievement, he seeks alternative ways to teach and test students.

Leadership can be discussed in terms of its effects. Typically, leadership either reinforces the existing structures or promotes change through dialogue and collaboration. Effective leaders evaluate the needs of the group. As those needs change, these leaders provide appropriate support for making adjustments to those changes. Culturally proficient leaders help the school's faculty and staff assess its culture and determine how the school affects the students and its community. They develop strategies for resolving conflict effectively and for addressing the dynamics of difference within the school. In shaping the school's formal and nonformal curriculum, they include information about the heritage, lifestyles, and values of all people in society.

In the urban center of the same county as Rolling Meadows, Coolidge Middle School Principal Richard Diaz is also ready to conduct a needs assessment. The school's student demographics had changed from virtually all African American to about one fourth Latino in less than 5 years. Furthermore, his urban district includes about 70% Latino students. Among the many changes he has initiated at the elementary school is to provide instruction in Spanish to all students. This not only provides those whose primary language is Spanish the opportunity to develop bilingual skills in both their native tongue and their new language (English), but it also offers native English speakers the chance to learn Spanish to prepare to function in multilingual settings as teenagers and adults. His vision helps African American students learn about the lifestyles of the Spanish-speaking students, and it mitigates any pressures that could result from having two languages spoken in the school.

Unfortunately, such exemplary leadership is rare. Too often, as schools become increasingly African American or Latino, district administrators fail to provide adequate support for leaders to make systemic interventions in the schools. If these leaders then fail to reverse or to stop a downward trend, the district administrators blame the students, their families, or their cultures—or perhaps the principals—for the continuing problems.

Valverde and Brown (1988) describe the problems faced by minority school administrators. They must

> demonstrate loyalty to superiors, fellow administrators, and teachers; explain dysfunctional practices of school districts in the education of minorities; and help district personnel to understand what is important to minority groups. All the while they serve as agents of change on behalf of policies and practices considered appropriate to the enhancement of minority children and youth. (p. 152)

As teachers, administrators, and educational consultants, we have seen that culturally proficient leadership can be exercised well by anyone, independent of gender, ethnicity, social class, sexual orientation, or physical or sensory ability. Those who are effective are most often formal leaders who know how to use the talents of nonformal leaders. They have a vision of what education at the school can be for all students, they can communicate that vision to others, and they have the knowledge and skills to work with others to assess the school's needs and to devise ways of providing for student needs in achieving their shared vision.

HISTORICAL CHANGES IN SCHOOL LEADERSHIP

Another key attribute of culturally proficient leaders is their awareness of the historical context of contemporary education. The schools in our country today are the result of many historical processes. The political, economic, and cultural context has influenced many of the changes in schools, such as the increasingly inclusive nature of education, from exclusively educating wealthy white boys to providing education for children of all socioeconomic strata, girls, and children of color. Many of our educational policies and practices have similarly interacted with the institutions and events of the wider society.

As you read this section, note that few of the numerous disquieting practices were instituted with malevolent forethought—which is precisely what often makes them difficult to expunge from current practice. Each of the systems described in this section evolved and was implemented so that society could accommodate new student populations. In most cases, the systems were borrowed from prevailing practices in business and industry. Each system or practice was adopted and implemented to provide ways for educating children for whom the schools were not originally designed while continuing to benefit the power brokers who made policies and controlled decision making.[1] In this section, we describe how some current practices became part of everyday schooling in our country so that we may understand current practice.

Table 3.2 gives a topical look at how organization specialists view modern organizational theory. We have included practices from those periods that can be found in most schools today. The first column identifies the management theory predominant during each period. The second column lists some of the educational practices associated with the corresponding periods. The third column illustrates the corresponding effect on women, cultural minority groups, gay men and lesbians, and the differently abled.

Classical Scientific Management and the Melting Pot

In judging the contributions to education from the classical scientific period to the present, we must take note of who attended schools at the turn of the century and for what purpose.

TABLE 3.2 Management Theory and Its Influence on Today's Schools

Management Periods	Traditional Practices	Approach to Diversity
Classical period of scientific management, 1890s-1930s	Organizational charts, tracking, testing	Schools teach basic subjects to most students; high schools allocate students to socioeconomic classes based largely on racial ethnic castes
Human relations period, 1930s-1950s	Site-level processes, role of principal	More students from diverse socioeconomic groups attend school; class and caste still affect the quality of the education offered
Organizational behavior period, 1950s-1970s	Schools as social systems	School desegregation further mixes students of various castes and classes; students are expected to improve academic performance because of with whom they attend school
Modern period, 1980s-present	Diversity as a dynamic	Schools attempt to develop programs and use approaches that address the educational needs of all students

Compulsory attendance laws, where they existed, usually required attendance only through the sixth or eighth grade. Also at this time, schools were deeply involved in helping to Americanize immigrants, the vast majority of whom were from eastern and southern Europe. Chiefly, schools' function in society was to provide labor for U.S. factories and farms. Within two or three generations, these immigrants were fluent in English, in many cases had Anglicized their names, and were considered full-fledged U.S. citizens. For these people, the metaphor for this process of cultural assimilation is often termed the *melting pot*. For them, the term was accurate and descriptive; within two to three generations, they did blend into the increasingly diverse United States. In ever-greater numbers, they moved into professions and other jobs for which high school and college education were needed. The part of our legacy that is often overlooked is that people from African, Latin American, Native American, and Asian and Pacific

Island cultures would not melt into this emerging new United States. Through personal initiative, many individuals were to become economically successful in this country, but more often than not, most were blocked from progress in schools and places of employment.

Today, most school districts require compulsory attendance through high school. Schools in urban centers and isolated rural settings are increasingly populated by African American and Latino students. These students simply will not assimilate into U.S. society the way that European American students did. African American and Latino students continue to populate lower-tracked classes disproportionately, drop out early from high school, and perform below norms on standardized tests (Hodgkinson, 1991; Kozol, 1991; Oakes, 1985). We are now grappling with how to provide at least a high school education for all students, and those attempts have met with a mixture of successes and failures. During the past generation or two, our society has explained the failures of lower socioeconomic African American and Latino students in terms of their disadvantaged or deprived nature—factors internal to them or to all cultures. Instead, we must examine our assumptions about the factors external to them, what they bring to school, and what we need to do differently to be successful in teaching all students (Freire, 1970; Sleeter & Grant, 1991).

Another artifact from the classical scientific management period is standardized testing. Wiggins (1989) notes that "tests grew out of the 'school efficiency' movement in the years between 1911 and 1916" (pp. 704-705). Further, "the reformers then, as now, were far too anxious to satisfy external critics and to reduce complex intellectual standards and teacher behaviors to simple numbers and traits" (p. 705).

> Implicitly there were signs of hereditarian and social-class based views of intelligence; the tests were used as sorting mechanisms at least partly in response to the increased heterogeneity of the school population as a result of the influx of immigrants. (p. 705)

Standardized testing and its consequent system of student tracking for instruction is an artifact of the classical scientific management period. Testing and tracking were designed to lead students straight to the careers for which their socioeconomic classes predestined them.

As Ogbu (1978; Ogbu & Matute-Bianchi, 1990) and others point out, African Americans, Latinos, Native Americans, and Asians are not likely to melt into a uniformly European American society. Such an occurrence is not only improbable but also undesirable. At the turn of the century, issues of culture, social class, gender, and ability were different for school policymakers and practitioners than they are for their counterparts today. Today, the challenge is to define a system that provides opportunities for people of diverse cultural, social class, gender, and physical and sensory ability backgrounds to receive an education enabling them to take their rightful positions in a world that now values labor of the mind more than that of the strong back. In such a setting, all forms of school testing should be examined in terms of their ability to measure student achievement authentically, as well as to facilitate development of effective instructional strategies.

We have good news and bad news about the challenges our nation faces. The good news is that we are doing a better job of addressing issues of diversity than we ever have, and we are doing better than any other nation in the world. The bad news is that no one else is doing any better than—or even as well as—we are. The really good news, though, is that if we do this well, if we can rise and meet this challenge, we will be better prepared than anyone to meet the demands of our increasingly global economy and interconnected world community.

Winston Alexander, Rolling Meadows assistant superintendent for business, is reviewing the proposals he received in response to the RFP and is learning a lot. He gets some information from the specific responses to the questions the RFP team proposes, but the team gleans even more insight from the underlying values of the consultants. It is easy to discern what the consultants believe from the way they present themselves and in the extra materials they include. Right now he muses over two ideas:

- No nation has ever undertaken to provide universal education for as broad a spectrum of social class and ethnic and racial groups as has the United States.

- We are more successful at education than any nation in the world today, but our development of a de facto caste system has created great inequities. We are at a point in history where we must heed the warning to avoid creating "two societies, separate and unequal" (Riot Commission, 1968).

Changes in the Way We Do Business

The human relations, organizational behavior, and modern organizational periods have spawned major changes in the way private companies do business. Corporations search for more effective ways to use their workers due to both the pressures from labor unions and the realization that increasingly complex companies need more highly skilled workers. Schools have been affected by the same evolutionary trends that businesses have.

In the human relations period, managers viewed workers as people who could be motivated through intrinsic systems because they had the inner desire to do well (McGregor, 1960). During the organizational behavior period, managers started examining companies not only in terms of organization charts but also in terms of the organic culture of the workplace (Deming, 1986; Drucker, 1954). During the modern period, managers have acknowledged that the labor force and consumer populations are becoming increasingly diverse and that having a well-educated diverse workforce is in the best interests of U.S. businesses (Boaz & Crane, 1985; Hodgkinson, 1991). Schools have adopted these new organizational practices in very uneven ways throughout the country. In fact, one would be hard-pressed to go into any school without finding vestiges of the classical scientific management period alongside more modern practices.[2]

Whatever term future educational scholars use to define the period of the 1980s and 1990s, this epoch will probably be distinguished by great and growing disparities between white children and children of color and between children from middle-income families and those from lower-income ones. It will be defined by whether educational reform programs are implemented systemically to ensure the social and educational successes of children without regard to their culture, different ability, gender, or family income. These systemic reforms will have to include our examination of our own assumptions about these groups, which are embedded in our curricular, instructional practices, as well as in how we use data to inform our decision-making processes.

If we are to confront this moral dilemma successfully, we must collaborate with other culturally proficient school leaders. Today's uneducated and undereducated citizens have fewer opportunities to enjoy the bounties of this country as compared with their predecessors in earlier generations. Education has become increasingly central to attaining material comforts in modern society. We are now striving to educate the vast majority of the population. The commitment to educate children independent of their ethnicity, social class, gender, or different physical or sensory ability must be predicated on the belief in their capacity to learn. Our task is to determine how to provide the relevant, needed education.

One way we can do this is to recognize the importance of the theories of leadership and organization that underlie our behavior. Understanding your role as a culturally proficient leader in this context provides you with a clearer sense of how organizations work and why they sometimes do not work. In the next chapter, we discuss why change is so difficult in some organizations and what culturally proficient leaders can do about it.

NOTES

1. The dynamic of entitlement is fully explained in Chapter 5.
2. In Chapter 4, we discuss how having school personnel and social policies derived from various value sets complicates the job for school leaders.

FOUR

Overcoming Resistance to Change

At Coolidge Middle School, Derek effectively teaches children from diverse ethnic and socioeconomic backgrounds, but down the hall, Brittney, a second year teacher, is very unsuccessful with and unhappy about having to teach "that kind of child," referring to various children from the local community. DeLois, Kareem, and several other teachers here organize their students by reading levels, continuously moving children to the next highest reading level as they progress through the year. By June, their top groups are quite large. On the other hand, Brittney is among the many teachers in the school who organize reading levels at the beginning of the year and keep the students in the same groups all year long, regardless of how much individual students progress.

In the faculty meeting room, Fernando, the vice principal of curriculum and climate, writes on the board, "That men do not learn very much from the lessons of history is the most important of all the lessons that history has to teach. Aldous Huxley, 1959."

"There he goes again," Harvey whispers to Lane. Fernando has developed a mantra of change and a rallying cry for the new order of things he is trying to establish at Coolidge Middle School. He knows that one speech, one memo, or one staff meeting will not do it. Every time the faculty and staff members see him, Fernando talks about change and what it will mean for whomever he is addressing, as well as how it will affect the students and the school's community.

"These diversity staff development meetings are a waste of time," Harvey continues. "No one's going to change. I've been here for 17 years, and I've seen it all. I have tenure, so I'll just sit tight. These VPs are only here until they get a promotion. Each one brings his own program, and each program leaves with the VP. If I wait long enough, I won't have to do a thing."

Across the room, DeLois and Kareem have been eagerly taking notes. "I wish I had taken more history courses when I was in college," DeLois sighs. "I'm sure that I could be more effective if I had a stronger historical foundation for what we are doing."

"We're not here to teach history, we're here to teach kids," Kareem retorts. "I wish he would just tell us more about this cultural proficiency model so I could figure out what I have to do in my classroom."

"You're right," Ellie pipes in. "Fernando just needs to mandate what he wants done. Understanding history is not going to change some of the bigots in this room."

In this book, we present cultural proficiency as an effective way to respond to the issues of diversity in your school. We look at the concepts of leadership and schools as systems to help you understand why and how educators approach educational and social challenges as they do. We also outline the approaches of a culturally proficient educational leader. In this chapter, we explain the change process and identify basic activities in which you, as a school leader and a change agent, must engage to facilitate a successful change in your classroom, school, or district.

The primary barriers to cultural proficiency are the presumption of entitlement and unawareness of the need to adapt (Cross et al., 1989). People with a *presumption of entitlement* believe that they have acquired all the personal achievements and societal benefits they have accrued solely on their own merit and character, and therefore don't feel a need to release or reorder any societal or organizational perquisites they may have. *Unawareness of the need to adapt* means failing to recognize the need to make personal and school changes in response to the diversity of the people with whom one interacts simply because it never occurred that there was a problem. People who are unaware of the need to adapt often believe that if the others, the newcomers, change or adapt to the environment, there will be no problems. They have not yet come to understand that once the commitment to cultural proficiency is made, everyone changes to create a new school culture.

As a culturally proficient leader, you will have to seek ways to address and overcome these barriers as you introduce the concept of cultural proficiency to other educators. In doing so, you will face varying reactions to your change message. You will find some people very eager to use the model, but others will neither want to change nor understand why you want them to.

You will also find that even when people want to change, they show some resistance to the change process. That's natural. For all of us, change requires some loss: We must give up some aspect of our current self-perception and our well-practiced modus operandi. When we are asked to make the changes necessary to address the diversity-related issues in our programs effectively, we may feel threatened both psychically and politically. As you lead fellow educators toward cultural proficiency, you will have to find ways to help them get past these feelings and overcome their resistance to change. This chapter offers specific strategies to guide you in these tasks. Before doing so, however, we follow Huxley's admonition to avoid repeating the mistakes of the past by seeking some understanding of historical changes in how schools have responded to diversity.

CHANGING RESPONSES TO DIVERSITY

Major Social Movements

Societal response to diversity has changed a lot in the past 50 years. Each decade has spawned new social policies in response to the current issues of concern. Schools have responded to these changes as well. If we are to understand the forces of policy evolution and the multiple factors that have led to policy shifts in U.S. society, particularly in schools, we must track the development of social policies related to the issues of diversity, the major movements in schools, and the concomitant resistance to these changes. The major social movements of the past 50 years are as follows:

Before 1950s: Segregation

1950s: Desegregation

1960s: Integration, equal access, equal rights

1970s: Equal benefits, multiculturalism

1980s: Diversity

1990s: Cultural competence

2000s: Cultural proficiency

Prior to the 1950s: Segregation

Before the 1950s, legal separation of cultural and racial groups in the United States was the norm. We can easily recognize this separation because it has been defined in legal terms in our country's history. In the southern United States, legal forms of segregation included slavery and Jim Crow laws, which defined discrete races, mandated the separation of those races in public settings (e.g., buses and restaurants), and dictated extremely different ways of treating individuals based on their identified race. Both slavery and Jim Crow systems were based on legislative decisions by southern states and upheld by state and federal court review. The remanding of Native Americans to reservations is another example of actions taken by federal and state legislatures, courts, and chief executives. To denigrate Native American people further, white people uprooted many and moved them to even less desirable locations when they discovered valuable mineral deposits or otherwise coveted property. Formally beginning with the Mexican Cession of 1848 (though the encroachment had been under way for well over a century), native residents of what is now the southwestern United States were often excluded from the political and economic mainstream and increasingly marginalized as European Americans emigrated into this area.

For Asians, the Chinese Exclusion Acts of 1882 and 1902 were federal legislative acts supported by the executive and judicial branches of our government. These acts of Congress were specifically designed to control and minimize Asian immigration once Asians were no longer needed in labor-intensive projects such as building railroads throughout the western United States. Another example of legally sanctioned segregation is Executive Order 9066, initiated by President Franklin D. Roosevelt and supported by Congress and the U.S. Supreme Court, which herded U.S. citizens of Japanese ancestry into relocation camps during World War II.

The 1950s: Desegregation

The 1954 *Brown v. Topeka Board of Education* decision that ended segregation in public facilities had its genesis in countless legal initiatives. Eight years before the Brown decisions, President Harry S. Truman issued an executive order to desegregate the military. As we all know, it has taken the half century since Truman's order to desegregate the military. (Even now, there is a compelling argument that although the command structure has been desegregated, African Americans, Latinos, and other U.S. citizens of low socioeconomic status are overrepresented among the front-line combatants who take the greatest casualties during conflict.)

Throughout our country's history, disenfranchised groups have used the courts and the legislatures to seek redress of their grievances. The *Brown* decisions are widely acknowledged to have been the civilian apex of those efforts. Though the *Brown* decisions officially ended segregation, actual segregation did not end in all places for all times. To this day, *de facto* segregation (observed segregation, which does not result from legal mandates such as Jim Crow laws) continues. Nonetheless, the *Brown* decisions have provided us with the tools by which we have been able to begin the legal process of dismantling segregation policies and practices that permeate every region of this country.

The process of school desegregation has been fraught with problems from the very beginning. Despite many successes in which children have benefited from school desegregation (Hawley, 1983), public attention has chiefly been focused on cases of resistance and failure. In southern states, private academies quickly emerged to offer segregated alternatives to European American students. Throughout the country, European American (and increasingly middle-class African American, Latino, and Asian Pacific Islander American) families have fled to suburbs to escape unwanted school assignments in urban areas. In some cases, these parents did not want to have their children attend a school outside their neighborhood, but in many cases, parents simply wanted to isolate their children from children with cultural backgrounds different from their own. Often, they viewed different children as genetically or culturally inferior to themselves. In response, the children and parents who were the targets of these reactions felt alienated from the dominant culture.

The 1960s: Integration, Equal Access, Equal Rights

The shift from desegregation to integration and equal access and rights was monumental. The 1960s was the decade of domestic revolutions. There were sit-ins, love-ins, bra burnings, freedom rides, and insurrection in the urban centers. It was a period of social justice activism, with the push for civil rights expanding from the southern states and broadened to include other cultural groups and women.

In schools, the push to desegregate had two consequences. First, voluntary and mandatory school desegregation efforts were designed to provide African American children and youth the same opportunities that white children and youth were receiving. Second, the expansion of entitlement programs (e.g., Title I of the Elementary and Secondary Education Act and the Emergency School Assistance Act) led to many African American children and youths being placed in programs for the disadvantaged. The unintended consequence of these programs is that the labels became affixed, and students more often than not received a poor education. It was during this time that educators first started to become aware of research on teacher expectations, gender bias, and second language instruction.

The 1970s: Equal Benefits and Multiculturalism

During this period, diverse U.S. citizens were striving to extend the legal gains won during previous decades to broader societal contexts, such as the workplace. As educators were increasingly confronting children of diverse cultural experiences, they needed new approaches, strategies, and techniques for teaching; thus, the educational emphasis on multiculturalism was spawned. Multiculturalism represents a departure from the assimilationist model, which had worked well for eastern and southern Europeans but was not working well for people in communities of color. In addition, many educators questioned the appropriateness of assimilation for people of every cultural group, even those people who readily left behind their own distinctive cultures and melted into the U.S. mainstream. During this period, women's issues entered the multiculturalism discussion in many schools. In the broader society, gay men and lesbians were beginning to assert their rights to equal societal opportunities and benefits.

The 1980s: Diversity

During this era, corporate America discovered that it was good business to address diversity-related issues. Many companies began offering diversity training for managers and other employees, and many began developing distinctive marketing strategies to target various sectors of society. As with most things, however, businesses did not uniformly embrace diversity throughout all companies or even throughout all industries. For instance, the banking and the automobile sectors have recognized the money to be made in these new markets, but the technology sector still appears to be lagging far behind. Similarly, while the leaders in some companies bristled at the mere suggestion of diversity training, others enthusiastically plunged into it. During this period, the aspects of diversity included in this training were also expanded from race, ethnicity, and gender to include issues of sexual orientation, disability, and age.

The 1990s and Beyond:
Cultural Competence and Cultural Proficiency

University hospitals, child care resources, and advocacy agencies have made strides to make a difference for their employees and their clients. In schools, the efforts of Comer (1988), Levin (1988), Sizer (1985), and Slavin (1996) appear to be consistent with the basic tenets of cultural proficiency. They believe that all children and youth can learn and, without arguing the relative merits of school desegregation, illustrate that children can learn well in their own neighborhoods. Although the national debate over school desegregation has not ended, it now focuses on the equitable distribution of human and capital resources.

Key Aspects of Major Social Movements

Now that we have provided a historical overview of the move toward cultural proficiency, we are ready to delve into how these social movements have affected social policy, the social impetus for these policies, the contemporary labels given to historically oppressed persons during this period, and the responses of these persons to discrimination. Table 4.1 organizes these various aspects of the major social movements of the past 50 years.

Relative Time Period

Look at the Relative Time Period column of Table 4.1 and find the decade during which you turned 10 years old.[1] Imagine for a moment the conversations you heard and the news reports you remember about diversity issues from that time of your life, and

TABLE 4.1 Evolution of Equity Policies

Relative Time Period	Social Policy	Motivation and Social Impetus	Label for Historically Oppressed People	Effects of Discrimination
Before 1950s	Segregation	Legal separation	Genetically, culturally inferior	Alienation
1950s	Desegregation	Legal	Deprived	Dissonance
1960s	Integration, equal access, equal rights	Legal activism for social justice	Disadvantaged	Marginality
1970s	Equal benefits, multiculturalism	Education	Deficient	Dualism
1980s	Diversity	Economic	Different	Negotiation
1990s	Cultural competence	Moral	Diverse	Bicultural affirmation
2000s	Cultural proficiency	Ideal	*En la Kech*[a]	Multicultural transformation

[a] This is a Mayan term for "I am in you and you are in me." We thank our colleague, Alberto Ochoa of San Diego State University, for his contributions to this table.
The initial draft of this table was devised with input from our colleagues John Browne, Alberto Ochoa, and Susan Taira.

then look at the Social Policy column. You might remember the events that informed the social policy listed in that column.

The Relative Time Period column represents the approximate decade of each social policy period. This column is best understood by notable events. The 1954 *Brown v. Topeka Board of Education* decision by the U.S. Supreme Court effectively brought an end to the legal basis for segregation. The 1964 Civil Rights Act introduced desegregation, which evolved into integration and a push for equal rights and equal access. As a result of school integration during the 1960s, by the 1970s, educators recognized that they were not prepared to teach children from different cultural groups; they needed both information about these groups and new educational skills and strategies suited to these groups to teach effectively. The 1980s ushered in a focus on managing schools more effectively, and schools began to adopt the organizational development language and tools used for enhancing the economic viability of businesses. The failure of these social policies to make significant and lasting changes in the United States has brought us to the moral imperative of the 1990s to focus on cultural competence as we look to the ideal of cultural proficiency in the 2000s.

BOX 4.1 Table 4.1, Columns 1 and 2	
Relative Time Period	Social Policy
Before 1950s	Segregation
1950s	Desegregation
1960s	Integration Equal access Equal rights
1970s	Equal benefits Multiculturalism
1980s	Diversity
1990s	Cultural competence
2000s	Cultural proficiency

Social Policy

The Social Policy column in Table 4.1 illustrates the evolution of equity policies as a result of societal forces. In that column, find the cell that best describes your focus and concerns today (or suggest a social policy describing your own focus and concerns). For some of us, our focus today is the same as the societal focus following the decade in which we turned 10 years old. For others, our focus has changed from what we remember being emphasized when we were 10.

In Table 4.1, the rows suggest movement across time, rather than fixed, rigid, discrete periods. Not everyone in society moved through each period simultaneously. Further, the social policies and their underlying attitudes and practices are cumulative; as society moves from one period to the next, it continues to include policies, attitudes, and practices from the previous periods. Many of us may continue to be guided by outdated policies, hold attitudes we acquired years ago, and implement long-standing practices in our work, home, and community interactions.

Motivation and Social Impetus

Just as policies, attitudes, and practices are cumulative, so is the motivation to change any particular policy. The social impetus and motivation for a particular decade may appear isolated, yet closer inspection may reveal that the motivating forces from previous decades have also been influential. Moreover, each

BOX 4.2 Table 4.1, Columns 1 and 3	
Relative Time Period	*Motivation and Social Impetus*
Before 1950s	Legal separation
1950s	Legal
1960s	Legal activism for social justice
1970s	Education
1980s	Economic
1990s	Moral
2000s	Ideal

social policy era spawns awareness in groups that did not initiate the change to press for social reforms affecting them, too. For example, the modern civil rights movement of the 1960s struggled to gain rights for African Americans and later for other cultural minority groups. These struggles then helped to spawn the modern reconvergence of both the feminist movement and the gay pride movement.

In Table 4.1, the Motivation and Social Impetus column lists the social impetus for the policy focus during each historical period. Briefly, the motivations and social impetuses for social policies of each period are as follows:

- The social impetus for the changes leading from segregation prior to the 1950s to desegregation and integration in the 1950s and 1960s focused on obtaining legal equity.

- During the 1960s, the social impetus continued to focus on legal equity, such as the provisions of the 1964 Civil Rights Act. In the push for integration, equal access, and equal rights, however, legal changes alone did not suffice. To broaden the application of these legal measures, the social impetus shifted to activism for social justice. For instance, such activism included the development of programs to rectify inequitable distribution of resources, such as nutrition, prenatal care, child care, and early childhood education.

- During the 1970s, the impetus for multiculturalism was almost uniquely motivated by the widely acknowledged need for equity in education. Educators sought to teach

---

language arts and social studies in ways that recognized and included the increasingly multicultural populations found in U.S. schools (Banks, 1994).

- During the 1980s, the motivation for social policies of diversity was primarily economic issues. The business community recognized the changing demographics of consumers and workers. Once businesspeople recognized that diversity has an economic payoff, they started to make many changes addressing this issue (e.g., changes in TV programming, images in commercials, and languages used in automatic teller machines).

- During the 1990s, educators and other community leaders began to view cultural proficiency as a moral imperative. This book is an outgrowth of this social impetus, because we recommend social policies and school reforms that reflect cultural proficiency. (We discuss the moral imperative for these social policies in Chapter 5.)

- For the 2000s and beyond, cultural proficiency is our ideal vision of what this society will become.

BOX 4.3 Table 4.1, Columns 1 and 4	
Relative Time Period	Label for Historically Oppressed People
Before 1950s	Genetically, culturally inferior
1950s	Deprived
1960s	Disadvantaged
1970s	Deficient
1980s	Different
1990s	Diverse
2000s	En la Kech

Labels for Historically Oppressed People

In Table 4.1 in the Label for Historically Oppressed People column, we list the progression of labels that have been ascribed to various nondominant groups in our society. These labels reflect the power of dominant groups to define others in relation to the norms set by the group in power, and to name them in such a way that their otherness is reinforced. Oppressed people (e.g., women, people of color, gay men and lesbians, the aged, and the differently abled) move through a progression of stages in reaction to both the social policies of the time and their current and historical position in society.

Note the progress from social Darwinist attributions of inferiority, deprivation, disadvantage, and deficiency to a recognition of difference without the negative connotations. The social Darwinist attributions are classic labels that blame oppressed people for their lot in life, even though these groups of people have been legally, educationally, and economically discriminated against. All disenfranchised and oppressed groups move through this system of being reclassified by the dominant society.

Across time, each cultural group has been assigned the same labels from the dominant society. In each case, the group labels were pernicious, and the societal response by each group was feelings of alienation from the dominant society. Prior to the 1950s, slavery and Jim Crow laws gave widespread sanction to the belief that African Americans were genetically and culturally inferior, despite the numerous instances of free blacks making significant academic and economic accomplishments throughout U.S. history. During this period, the dominant society also commonly segregated black communities from white ones.

Similarly, most Native Americans were confined to reservations either by legal mandate or through economic disincentives for leaving the reservations. Though many Native Americans have built strong independent lives either separate from or within the dominant society, the vast majority have been treated by the dominant society as culturally and genetically inferior. As with African U.S. citizens, the labels of inferiority are often cloaked in seemingly beneficent terms describing (and treating) them as exotic. Although society is generally too sophisticated to use such terms as *noble savage* any more, it is not unusual for schools to invite Native Americans to dance and tell folk stories, with little regard for learning the societal and spiritual similarities and differences among cultural groups.

For Latino groups in general, and U.S. citizens of Mexican ancestry in particular, state laws that forbade children from speaking Spanish in schools heightened Latinos' alienation from the dominant society. Similarly, the various Asian groups that immigrated to this country were segregated into urban communities or labor camps. By prohibiting the immigration of their compatriots, the dominant society continuously reminded Asian Americans of their second-class status. Clearly, African American, Native American, Mexican American, and Asian American feelings of alienation from the dominant society are not difficult to recognize and understand in this context of legally sanctioned segregation and exclusion.

During the 1950s, 1960s, and 1970s—periods of great social change—the labels for historically oppressed groups subtly shifted from *inferiority* to *deficiency*. Inferior people were easy to provide for. They were simply incapable of being like members of the dominant society. They were encoded as deviant, stupid, hostile, docile, childlike, or just plain backward. As society was moving into an era of having more of these groups in the social mainstream, however, different ways of experiencing them had to be developed.

Though referring to a person as *deficient* is hardly positive, it acknowledges a potential member of society. In fact, if it were not for a deficiency or two, these deficient persons could be just like members of the dominant society. Throughout this country, schools and other social agencies began to take the approach that because we were going to have to work with these groups, we had to figure out what was wrong with them and to provide what they needed. It was widely held that the unidentified deficiencies could be cured through remediation via public education.

Unfortunately, this perspective led to self-fulfilling prophecies in which we asked, How could we possibly educate people with these insurmountable deficiencies? The educational tracking system became the vehicle by which inordinate numbers of African Americans, Latinos, and other people with low socioeconomic status were placed into lower-ability groups and continuously exposed to basic academic skills. Throughout this period, few policymakers ever asked themselves this question: Why do some children of color, girls, and low-income children throughout the United States succeed in schools, and what conditions contributed to their success? The few policymakers who did, however, often reached an unfortunate answer: Success stories are meaningless anomalies.

At last, during the 1980s and 1990s, we have begun to use the terms *different* and *diverse*, which acknowledge a common valuing of one another as fellow humans. Perhaps in the third millennium we will begun to use terms such as the Mayan expression *en la Kech*, which signifies that "you are in me and I am in you"

BOX 4.4 Table 4.1, Columns 1 and 5	
Relative Time Period	*Effects of Discrimination*
Before 1950s	Alienation
1950s	Dissonance
1960s	Marginality
1970s	Dualism
1980s	Negotiation
1990s	Bicultural affirmation
2000s	Multicultural transformation

and extends a high level of humanity to the discussion of policy and equity. To paraphrase a provocative question asked by Joel Barker (1996), a futurist: What seems impossible to do today but if we could do it would radically change how we create equity across cultural groups? In 1950, the vast majority of people in this country probably could not have envisioned the changes that were to be made in human rights. Perhaps in the third millennium, people will accept as commonplace matters of equity beyond our imagination now.

Effects of Discrimination

In Table 4.1, the final column, Effects of Discrimination, reflects how historically oppressed people have internally responded to discrimination and to the labels ascribed to them. As the social policies, motivations, and labels changed, the attitudes, feelings, and beliefs of historically oppressed people changed in response. Prior to the 1950s, while isolated and segregated from the dominant culture, they experienced intense feelings of alienation. During this time, everyone in society agreed that there were an US and a THEM, and everyone knew to which group he or she belonged.

As society began to invite some historically oppressed people to assimilate into the dominant culture, they were expected to disassociate themselves from all vestiges of their primary or native culture, so they felt dissonance. Within the dominant culture, they faced tremendous obstacles and difficulties, yet they were obliged to resist reliance on their native cultural resources to help them overcome these problems. They knew that to be accepted into the dominant culture, they had to abandon all traces of their native culture. Similarly, they were expected to adopt the dominant culture's view, disparaging their native culture and denigrating the people in their native cultural group. Thus, they felt dissonance not only with members of the dominant culture and in settings reflective of the dominant culture, but also with members of their native culture and in settings reflecting their native culture (Adams, 1996; Kovel, 1984; Locust, 1996; McCarthy, 1993; Ogbu, 1978).

Many U.S. citizens who had emigrated from Europe were able to overcome these obstacles, as their distinctive native cultures melted into the dominant culture. Similarly, gay men and lesbians were able to assimilate as long as they carefully avoided being open about their sexual orientation. Even some women were able to assimilate by accepting the dominant society's definitions of gender roles: If they wished to become chief executive officers (CEOs), they accepted that they must dress, speak, and act like CEOs—that is, like white men (Boyd, 1984; Gilligan, 1983; Weiss & Schiller, 1988).

The melting pot did not work for all people, however. Some people, no matter how thoroughly they abandoned their own native culture, were still not welcomed into the dominant culture, as their physical appearance continued to distinguish them despite their best efforts at being indistinguishable. For instance, most women and people of color continue to look different from white men, even when they adopt the same values, attitudes, and behavior that white men show. Further, much to the surprise of some members of the dominant society, many historically oppressed people rejected entirely the goal of assimilation: They did not want to have their differences melted away.

During the 1960s, many people outside the dominant culture experienced feelings of *marginality:* They knew two cultures but were not entirely accepted by members of either one essentially because they could function in the other culture. Among those who experienced marginality were children bused to schools where very few members of their own primary group were present; once they learned to cope with and thrive in the dominant culture, they often felt marginalized on returning to their home communities. They no longer felt at home while at home. Similarly, Latino children forced to speak only English in school, to the point of forgetting or becoming developmentally disabled in their native language, feel marginalized in Latino culture. Native American Indian children educated in the long-running Bureau of Indian Affairs boarding schools too often fit neither in the white culture, for which they were educated, nor in their home cultures, from which they had been separated. In all these cases, the insult added to the injury was that these children continued to be marginalized in the dominant culture while being marginalized in their native cultures (Cummins, 1990; Duchene, 1990).

During the 1970s, many people were able to integrate success-fully into a new culture while remaining comfortable in their native culture. Nonetheless, they felt unable to mesh the two worlds, so they experienced a sense of *dualism*. Unlike marginal-ized people, who live between two worlds, people who feel dualism live in the two worlds, moving back and forth yet never carrying one into the other. Many adults experience a sense of dualism: They function successfully in corporate America yet continue to go home to a segregated community, where they socialize and worship with just the members of their native culture (Delpit, 1993; Fine, 1993; Sapon-Shevin, 1993).

During the 1980s, many people attempted to bring aspects of each culture into the world of the other. This process demands the skills of social and psychological negotiation, especially when the values and norms of the two cultures conflict with each other. Finally, starting in the 1990s, quite a few people have begun to feel bicultural (or multicultural) affirmation, functioning effec-tively in two or more cultural worlds such that each cultural world recognizes and respects their biculturality. Perhaps in the third millennium, people will experience multicultural transfor-mation, in which the norm for all people will be to know and function comfortably within several cultural groups (McCarthy, 1993; West, 1993; Willis, 1996).

In reviewing the changes across the past five decades, we can see historically oppressed people moving through a process of acceptance, internalization, and rejection of the labels given them by others and toward self-determinism and self-identification. Although the format presented here suggests that these general trends apply to all cultural groups, in fact, each cultural group moves at its own distinctive pace. Further, the individuals within each group vary widely in terms of how they view social policies, social impetuses and motivations, and labels, as well as in their responses to discrimination. For instance, even today, gay men and lesbians may experience feelings ranging from alienation to multicultural transformation. Newly immigrated Mexican Americans may still feel alienation, whereas their U.S.-born cousins may experience bicultural affirmation.

What does this historical process mean to the culturally proficient educational leader? It means that the culturally proficient leader has to be adept at recognizing that a typical school faculty comprises teachers, teacher aides, staff, counselors, and administrators who have had widely different life experiences. More important, the leader recognizes that the experiences of the school faculty and staff may be much different than the experiences of students and parents in the community served by the school. The culturally proficient leader recognizes that he or she must address issues of labeling in a way that helps dominant culture people understand the pain caused by labeling and helps recipients of such labeling go beyond that pain to focus on self-determination and self-identification.

CONFRONTING RESISTANCE TO CHANGE

As a culturally proficient leader, you may view each challenge to change as a welcome opportunity for growth, but for many of the people you lead, such a challenge is a threat to what is comfortable and familiar. Throughout the change process, you must continually bear in mind three goals, which sometimes may seem to conflict, but which are all essential to effective and productive change:

1. Create an environment where people are comfortable and motivated to do their work.
2. Point out aspects of the environment that demand change.
3. Avoid demoralizing the people who will be required to change.

As you implement the strategies for change described in this section, try to think of ways in which the preceding goals will influence how you do so.

TABLE 4.2 Managing Transitions

Phase of the Change Process	*Characterized by These Emotions*	*Individual Challenges*	*Organization Challenges*
Release the old **Endings**	Denial, shock Anger, hostility Elation, relief	Accept the reality of change Release attachment to the old ways of doing things	Create the need for change
Transition **Change**	Resistance Sabotage Depression Support Facilitation	Disconnect from the past Overcome resistance Commit to the future Connect with the transition	Communicate a vision of the future Dismantle old systems Mobilize commitment to the new vision Stabilize transition management
Transition **Beginnings** *Embrace the new*	Fear Exploration Resolution Commitment Excitement	Master new routines Learn new cultural norms Embrace the new organizational climate	Institutionalize the change Reward and reinforce the new systems

Adapted from Beckhard and Harris (1987).

Steps for Implementing Change

The change process is complex. When culturally proficient leaders create learning environments in their schools, their entire faculty and staff participate in the process of assessing the need for and implementing change. The basic steps in any change process are beginning, middle, and end. Culturally proficient leaders implement the steps in the appropriate order: ending, by releasing the old paradigms; transitioning between the old and the new; and beginning to use new behaviors and processes in a consistent way. Table 4.2 outlines the process.

We have found that most leaders add to people's resistance to change because of the order in which they introduce change and the aspects of the changing system on which they focus. Culturally proficient leaders understand that change begins by ending something. You end the way you have been doing things (e.g., your focus on similarities in the diversity program or your goal of cultural blindness). Even if your faculty has intellectually accepted cultural proficiency as the model for addressing issues of diversity, they will be more willing to move forward toward new goals if you acknowledge their losses and their need to grieve those losses.

DeLois is looking at her Heroes and Holidays calendar, which she has been so proud of. At the staff development session today, she learned that her approach of selecting one month each year to focus on a particular ethnic group was leading to cultural incapacity. She now understands that learning to say "Happy New Year" in Chinese and reading a story about Cesar Chavez will not significantly change the way the students interact with each other on the playground, and it probably will do nothing to raise scores on standardized tests. It has taken her years to collect costumes, recipes, and thousands of pictures—pictures of Chinese babies, African children, and families in the Brazilian rainforest. Now, as she packs them away, DeLois wonders how many parents she insulted by pointing proudly to the pictures saying, "We have a lesson on your people, so your child will be comfortable in our classroom."

Sighing deeply, DeLois places the box on the shelf.

Kareem walks into the classroom and notices DeLois's red-rimmed eyes. "Why are you so down? I thought you were gung ho on this cultural proficiency thing. You even volunteered to chair the policy examination committee."

"Well, I'm a little sad, Kareem. I hate to think that everything I've been doing all these years has been a waste."

"No, it hasn't been a waste. I never really understood your party approach to diversity, but I have noticed that you treat every child with respect, compassion, and the expectation that they will achieve. Then you make sure that they do by adjusting your style to their needs and abilities. I think that reflects your cultural proficiency more than this calendar and those recipes do."

"Thanks, Kareem," DeLois sniffs. "I guess this certificate of appreciation from the principal does say that some people noticed I was trying."

During the *endings* phase, culturally proficient leaders can facilitate the process by spending time with their staff members to acknowledge their feelings of perceived loss and by guiding the members of the school community through the stages of denial and shock, anger and hostility, and elation and grief (see Table 4.2). In this phase, the leader is challenging the school to create the need for change and the staff members to accept the reality of change. The culturally proficient leader develops a mantra of change and a rallying cry for the new order of things.

The *transition* period is marked by activities where people are no longer doing what they used to do, but they still aren't doing what they want to do. At this time, the leader introduces the new concepts and strategies and works to create a collective vision for how the school will be different as a result of this change. The leader then has the school dismantle the old systems and initiate most of the changes. Some people will be ready to participate immediately, others will be convinced that it won't work, and most will just sit back, waiting to see what happens. During this time, most people will try out new ideas yet revert back to old and comfortable ways of doing things.

The culturally proficient leader continues to challenge, encourage, and shepherd staff members forward while managing the transition. Many staff members complain and sing their songs of lament, foreboding, and ire. They resist, they sabotage, and they fall into depression. The culturally proficient leader remembers at this time that human beings do not change overnight. Children don't learn to read after one lesson, and adults don't learn new behaviors after one structured activity. Just as proficient teachers coach, support, and praise children for incremental improvements, culturally proficient leaders coach, support, and praise staff members as they try out new attitudes and new behaviors.

The *beginnings* of change come several months after the endings have been acknowledged and following the transition period. It is during the beginnings phase that the changes become institutionalized. It is also during this phase that resisters look for evidence that change is not working. Culturally proficient leaders are ready for the naysayers by explaining the process of making changes and setting realistic expectations for everyone. They are also prepared to point out where progress has been made. They find ways to reward the participants for their commitment to change and to reinforce the changes in the school. This is not, however, the time to stop and rest on one's laurels. Once one set of changes has been put in place and the systems within the school are supporting it, leaders look to see what else can be changed and how.

Principal Dina Turner is conducting a meeting with her site council. "We are at the midpoint of our year and our plan specifies that we are to assess our progress by examining our benchmarks. As you recall, our goals for this year were for schoolwide academic improvement in reading and for our learning more about our interaction patterns with students."

Bobby, one of her consistently unhappy teachers, replies, "You know, I am all for academic improvement, but I still don't see how it is related to having a teacher observing me in my classroom."

Another teacher, Celeste, speaks up in Dina's defense. "I am not sure that I can agree with you. I have noticed that the schoolwide focus on reading has made it easier to talk with my students about the recreational benefits of reading."

Grace Ishmael, a very active parent in the district adds, "That is a good point! Just this weekend my son asked if I didn't think that we watched way too much television. I hated to admit it, but he is right. I was just wondering how parents who are not members of the site council are reacting."

Dina says, "Obviously I am very supportive of our reading initiative. I am also deeply committed to our continued study of student-teacher interactions. Has anyone had the occasion to apply any of the research on teacher expectations in their classrooms?"

"Yes, I have," says Celeste. "You know, Bobby, I am confident that I am a good teacher, but those activities are really giving me insights to some of my blind spots. I am beginning to see how unintended behaviors can be so harmful!"

"What occurs to me," adds Dina, "is that if these behaviors occur between students and teachers, they must occur among adults too. I shudder at the thought!"

Grace has an idea. "You know, we may want to consider some of that training for parents. From what you are saying, it may be very enlightening, possibly a little uncomfortable, but very worthwhile."

"I do want to speak to the issue of discomfort," Dina replies. "Most teachers do not find the process uncomfortable. I believe if everyone sees themselves as students and are willing to commit the time and energy it takes to walk this avenue to improvement, we will all grow and our kids will really benefit. And, I agree, it would be good for this group too. It would be an excellent topic for training all our parents."

Overcoming Barriers of Resistance

With diversity programs, the first barrier of resistance is the unawareness of the need to change. Expect that people will attempt to assign blame and abdicate responsibility. Be prepared to hear,

"We didn't do anything to those people, why do we have to change?"
"This is America; they should be adapting to us."
"This is reverse discrimination."
"Why are we trying to fix something that's not broken?"

Culturally proficient leaders respond to this resistance in two ways: (1) They acknowledge the feelings of the complainers; change is seldom easy and is often unwanted, especially because a commitment to cultural proficiency means having to do more work. (2) They explain why the changes are being made: to serve the students and their families better. The plan is not to fix something that is broken; it is to grow as a school community for the students' benefit.

During the change process, conflict arises between the new ways and the old ways of doing things. The culturally proficient leader manages the resistance to change by using some of the strategies acquired when learning to manage the dynamics of difference (see Chapter 2); the techniques for managing the conflicts are similar. The culturally proficient leader ensures that the people being asked to change know that

- Change is not a way to punish anyone
- Change is consistent with the values and goals of the school
- Change is a vital part of a learning and growing organization
- Students and their families will be the primary beneficiaries of the change
- Faculty and staff will also benefit from working in a culturally proficient school

Each leader will meet a different type of resistance and must find appropriate ways of overcoming the resistance. We close this chapter by peeking over the shoulders of three change agents who have managed to overcome resistance in distinctive ways.

In Coolidge District, after principals Steve Petrossian, Richard Diaz, and Dina Turner hear that the board of education votes not to embrace cultural proficiency as a district policy, these administrators decide to make the guiding principles of cultural proficiency (see Chapter 2) their own value base for decision making. They regularly meet to offer one another support and encouragement in implementing their goals for cultural proficiency.

To move his school toward cultural proficiency, Steve carefully studies the essential elements of cultural proficiency (see Chapter 2) and then decides to start with the element valuing diversity because many of his staff members fervently resist any change. Their practices in the past have ranged from cultural incapacity to cultural blindness. Nonetheless, Steve has a couple of teachers (e.g., DeLois and Kareem) who truly value diversity and who are willing to chair committees that will develop ideas for manifesting a value for diversity on the campus.

Given the adamant resistance of his staff, Steve spends more time in the ending phase of managing transition (see Table 4.2). He has to make a case for change by showing the resisters how past behaviors have damaged students, the school's relationships with the community, and the school's reputation in the district. He then has to convince his teachers that the proposed change is integral to the school program, not just a supplement to it. After Steve implements the plan for integrating this element into his school system, he consults with faculty and staff to select another element for focus.

Richard Diaz, a middle school principal, is pleased to report that despite several false starts, he finally has had a number of celebrations as part of the food and fiestas program. Richard knows that this is only a superficial beginning, but it is all he can motivate his people to do. Initially, many of Richard's staff members resisted change because they perceived that to change meant that they had done something wrong or that their ideas and programs were no longer valued. After a conversation with his colleagues facilitated by the diversity consultant, all together are seeking new ways to address the issues of diversity. All participants are proud of what they are doing, and they are eager to do even more.

Richard knows that social events like the food and fiestas program were at best precompetent, but he knows that to be successful he has to create an environment where the faculty experience success. He makes a mental note to move quickly to more substantive activities.

Dina, the principal at the high school, has had a terrible year and is now facing some court recriminations. She is going to start with the element managing the dynamics of difference. Some of Dina's resisters declare that because they were not directly involved in any of the conflicts leading to the court battles, they should not be punished by having to attend workshops. Dina overcomes the resistance by reframing the situation. She points out that the workshops are not punishment, they are simply responding to changes in the school's culture that, heretofore, had not been acknowledged well. This is an opportunity to show students and parents what good teachers they are and how well they respond to their students' needs. All need to learn how to recognize conflicts caused by cultural differences, and all need to find appropriate ways to respond to them. Like Steve, Dina implements a plan for integrating this element into the school's culture and then works with faculty and staff to choose the next element on which to focus.

NOTE

1. Morris Massey (1979b) describes the process of identifying values by describing the social situation when you were 10 years old and the film series *What You Are Is Where You Were When. . .* By having people discuss what cells in the chart represent significant aspects of their lives, you bring alive the social history of the United States and reinforce the concepts the chart summarizes. In Activity 4.7, we describe the process for facilitating a discussion of Table 4.1 with staff.

FIVE

Understanding the
Barrier of Entitlement

Coolidge High School continues to be among the schools in the district and region that earn top academic honors. The advanced placement classes have fewer than 10% African American and Latino students. In the last 5 years, the Title I population has increased from 5% to 35%. In that same time period, the English as a second language (ESL) classes have increased from serving less than 2% of the student population to serving slightly more than 35% of the student population. There have been two resulting effects of these trends. The first has been decreased sections of honors classes and a dramatic increase in remedial and heterogeneous classes. The heterogeneous classes in English and social studies were created to overcome criticism about the negative effect of tracking; however, placement in mathematics and science classes has served to create levels among the English and social studies classes. The second effect of the demographic changes has been that the school's standardized test scores have steadily declined and have given the impression to the local media that the quality of education at the school has deteriorated. Teachers still have an interest in a traditional academic approach to curriculum. They also place a high value on a tracked system in which the highest achievers are allowed to move at an accelerated rate.

The extracurricular programs of the school, except for football and basketball, tend to be associated with cultural groups. Though the sports program is nominally integrated, swimming is perceived to be a white sport, wrestling a Latino sport, track an African American sport, and tennis an Asian Pacific Islander sport. Student government represents the demographic profile of the school, but most of the clubs and other organizations are predominated by one cultural group. Of the major cultural groups at the school, Latino students participate least in clubs and other organizations. In recent years, there has been tension among the groups. Some fights and retaliatory attacks have received wide coverage in the newspaper.

Bill Fayette, assistant superintendent of curriculum and instruction at Coolidge, has organized inservice training sessions for the faculty on cultural sensitivity that focus on the contributions of African Americans, Latinos, and Asian Pacific Islanders. As a result, a few teachers have organized culture clubs for students, and they are talking about developing elective ethnic studies courses.

For decades, educators and other leaders have recognized that an important step in creating change in schools is to identify barriers to the implementation of new ideas, programs, procedures, or techniques (Freire, 1970; Fullan, 1991; Giroux, 1992; Owens, 1995). In our view, cultural proficiency theory offers an excellent means for identifying these barriers, both in society in general and in the school setting in particular. The two primary barriers to cultural proficiency are (1) the presumption of entitlement, and (2) unawareness of the need to adapt. These barriers are manifest in the dominant society's view that the issues concerning people of color, women, and gay people are *their* problems, of little relevance to white males.

If you are to apply cultural proficiency theory to your school, you must thoroughly understand these barriers, particularly that of entitlement. For this reason, this chapter describes white male entitlement, which is the converse of the institutionalized forms of oppression—racism, sexism, ethnocentrism, and heterosexism—phenomena that penalize people for their membership in nondominant cultural groups. *Entitlement* is the accrual of benefits solely because of membership in a dominant group. Just as oppressed people are penalized because of their culture, other people benefit because of their membership in a privileged group within the dominant culture. If examined on a continuum, entitlement is the end at which some people (chiefly, heterosexual white men) have great power and control because of their membership in the dominant cultural group; *institutionalized oppression* is the other end, at which people (chiefly, people of color, women, and homosexuals) have relatively little institutionalized power or control because of their membership in a nondominant cultural group.

People seeking to shift the balance of power must understand their own distinctive role in ending oppression; which role they may play depends entirely on whether the cultural group to which they belong is the dominant one. For entitled people (dominant group members), their role requires a moral choice to assume personal responsibility and to take personal initiative. For oppressed people (nondominant group members), their role is to recognize oppression and to commit themselves to self-determination. In this chapter, we focus on the role of entitled persons. As a culturally proficient leader, you will surely need to guide both oppressed persons and entitled ones in assuming their distinctive roles. It is our view, however, that the more daunting challenge is to coach entitled persons in their roles. In addition, there are precious few materials available for guiding entitled persons, whereas there are now quite a few outstanding materials available for guiding oppressed persons from diverse cultural groups (Cheek, 1976; Gilligan, 1983; McIntosh, 1988; Vigil, 1980).

In this chapter, we describe the role of dominant group members, particularly the most entitled group members in our society, straight white men, in challenging the institutionalized forms of oppression and in creating culturally proficient schools where all members of the school's community have access to power and self-determination. One of the difficulties you will face is that most members of the dominant U.S. culture do not view themselves as more powerful or privileged than others in society, so they do not see themselves as stakeholders in these issues of power. Therefore, more often than not, entitled persons view issues of oppression and entitlement as issues for oppressed persons alone to worry about. In fact, the traditional manner of studying issues of equity and diversity (usually prescribed by persons from the dominant culture) is to study the powerlessness of people of color, women, and other oppressed groups.

Why don't discussions of diversity include white people and men? Entitlement. White people, and more particularly white men, choose—consciously or unconsciously—whether to participate actively in issues of equity and cultural proficiency. They may become angry, guilty, or indifferent to these topics. They may decry their forefathers' actions; they may protest that they never owned slaves; they may become depressed learning of some of the history that was never taught when they were students; or they may shrug it off and quietly declare that it is not their problem. The reality is that once entitled people react, they still can choose to address issues of power and to oppose acts that perpetuate oppression—or not. The first step in addressing these issues and opposing these actions is simply to acknowledge that the dynamics of entitlement do not accord people of color or women the same opportunity to choose whether to deal with issues of entitlement and oppression. These issues are part of their daily existence, just as power is an unacknowledged reality for white men.

To understand entitlement, we must understand how the empowered members of society are often oblivious to the ways in which they have benefited from their entitlement. Even when awareness dawns, they may still be reluctant to acknowledge the dynamics of race, gender, and sexual orientation, as well as socioeconomic class, in the expression of power. For instance, socioeconomics is clearly a major factor in determining who wields power in this country. Too often, however, the effects of poverty have blinded poor white people to the oppression experienced by other people based on their culture, especially people of color. As a result, impoverished white people often feel a disregard for—and even an antagonism toward—people of color. We study this concept more closely in the following section, which contrasts the migrant experiences of European Americans with those of immigrants from other parts of the world.

In this chapter, we introduce the concept of caste and discuss its role in U.S. history. We then describe various ways in which entitlement is manifested. Next, we discuss ways to recognize entitlement in schools, as well as some educational practices that reinforce entitlement and oppression. We close the chapter by describing how culturally proficient educators address entitlement and the moral issues related to it.

CASTE-LIKE STATUS AND OPPRESSION IN U.S. HISTORY

In discussing entitlement, we often use the terms *racism, ethnocentrism, sexism,* and *heterosexism,* all of which suggest heavy indictments. These terms are often confusing and frequently misused. As we continue to examine entitlement, we should be sure we share a common understanding of these terms. Racism has two components: (1) the belief that one ethnic group is superior to all others, and (2) the power to create an environment where that belief is manifested in the subtle or direct subjugation of the subordinate ethnic groups through a society's institutions. Ethnocentrism differs from racism in that it suggests a belief in the superiority of one's own ethnic group, but it says nothing about the group's power to subjugate other groups via societal institutions. Like racism, sexism and heterosexism have two components: (1) a belief that men and heterosexuals are superior to women and homosexuals, and (2) the power to institutionalize that belief, thereby subjugating women and homosexuals both overtly and covertly. When we know the definition of racism and other oppressive terms, we can more readily recognize how each of us fits into the social dynamics of racism and other forms of oppression.

The multitudinous effects of racism, ethnocentrism, sexism, and heterosexism permeate all aspects of people's lives in the United States. In addition, the effects of these oppressive forces are further complicated by the pervasive presence of a caste system. In this section, we discuss how socioeconomic status interacts with membership in nondominant cultural groups, thereby compounding an already complex issue.

Caste-Like Status Versus Immigrant Status

Our society is stratified by economic classes that overt U.S. values tell us are flexible and subject to change through hard work and determination. These classes are further stratified by the ethnic groups within them. Ogbu and Matute-Bianchi (1990) describe two types of ethnic minority status: immigrant status and caste status. Table 5.1 shows how Ogbu and Matute-Bianchi distinguish between immigrant and caste minorities. In U.S. society, *immigrant status* is a flexible category through which people have moved voluntarily, first choosing to immigrate and then choosing to assimilate, leaving behind their distinctive cultural membership and identification. People with immigrant status reinforce our belief in flexible strata in our society, because they frequently cross class boundaries, if not within a generation, then at least over several generations.

In contrast, *caste status* is an inflexible category in which a person's ethnic characteristics such as physical appearance and

TABLE 5.1 Types of Minority Status

	Immigrant Minorities	*Caste-like Minorities*
Definition	People who are assimilated into mainstream social and economic classes after one or two generations	People who, as a group, are prevented from moving out of the lowest social and economic classes
Reason for immigration	Moved voluntarily to the host society for economic, social, or political reasons	Were brought to host society involuntarily through slavery, conquest, or colonization
Characteristics	May be subordinated and exploited politically, economically, and socially Often successful in school May see themselves as "strangers" or "outsiders" May consider their menial position in this country to be better than what they had back home Do not internalize the negative effects of discrimination (as first-generation immigrants) Negative effects of discrimination not an ingrained part of their culture Affected by U.S. relations with country of origin: (1) worsening political ties between the country of origin and the host country lead to harsh treatment; (2) friendly political ties between the country of origin and the host country improve social and economic opportunities Biculturality and bilingualism are perceived as possible and acceptable	Remain involuntary and permanent minorities Believed to be unalterably inferior as a group Perception of inferiority perpetuated by myths and stereotypes depicting the group as lazy, sexually primitive, violent, aggressive, and disease ridden Formal and informal barriers to assimilation (e.g., prohibitions of intermarriage, residential segregation) created by host culture
Effects	Attitudes toward schooling that enhance strong desire for and pursuit of education Attitudes and behaviors that help them overcome barriers to education and high-status careers	Attitudes and behaviors that internalize host culture's perception of them Belief that schooling will not help them advance into the mainstream of society

SOURCE: Ogbu and Matute-Bianchi (1990).

language so differ from the dominant (white) caste that they prevent—or severely limit—that person's voluntary movement across class boundaries. For the rare individuals of lower castes who are able to cross class boundaries, caste continues to affect their status within their new social class. Thus, a person who has entered the middle class but belongs to a lower caste will be made to feel subordinate to other members of the middle class, who are of a higher caste. The existence of a caste system violates our fundamental U.S. belief in the ability to cross class boundaries at will. Most of us balk at the notion of a caste system in the United States, and we are tempted to reject even the possibility of its existence, just as we reject it as a concept that contradicts our fundamental values as a nation.

A History of Caste in the United States

The distinction between immigrant and caste minorities has been extremely important in the history of our country, and much of our society still functions in a caste system (Ogbu & Matute-Bianchi, 1990). Historically, our nation was founded by European immigrants, and as new generations of Europeans voluntarily migrated to this country, they moved through immigrant status en route to assimilation. Initially, the caste minorities were chiefly African and Native American Indian.

Even a rudimentary knowledge of history bears witness to how the experiences of immigrant versus caste minorities have differed. Basically, despite tremendous obstacles and much hard work, the second and subsequent generations of European immigrants were merged into the U.S. lifestyle. In contrast, African Americans and Native American Indians were prevented from entering the dominant culture by virtue of their caste. By ignoring the humanity of these outsiders, early European Americans readily justified both their encroachment on indigenous people, to steal their land, and their importation of slaves, to create a dirt-cheap labor pool for the colonists. Religious zealots often justified this savagery through their ethnocentrism. They neither understood nor appreciated the beliefs and behavior of the Africans and the Native American Indians, so they claimed it as their duty to civilize and Christianize these "primitive" people. They rationalized enslavement and brutalization as a means to a glorious end: converting these heathens to the Christian faith. Over time, the colonists institutionalized slavery and the practice of exiling Native American Indians to small parcels of land.

Following the war against the British, white men looked to British law and tradition to establish the U.S. government, society, and culture. These institutions formalized the political, social, and economic rights of landowning white men. These rights and influence were extended further through America's landmark court cases, governmental policies, and capitalist economic system. In the 1830s, Jacksonian democracy extended voting rights to nonlandowners, thereby expanding societal participation to other white men, members of the entitled caste. As new European immigrants arrived, if they were willing to work hard and to suffer many indignities, they—or at least their children or grandchildren—were granted entry into the dominant culture.

Meanwhile, racism became institutionalized in the new nation, and Native American Indians and African Americans were denied both the rights of citizenship and participation in the political and social life of the nation. Africans and African Americans were legally defined as being worth three fifths of a white person. Native American Indians were slaughtered through direct aggression, as well as by indirect means, such as exposing them to disease and preventing them from using their land to maintain their existence. Africans were enslaved first as chattel and then in a politically acceptable fashion, through Jim Crow laws, which carried the tacit legal sanction for mob violence against African Americans that included the threat to lynch with or without cause. Native American Indians were driven onto reservations and then moved again and again each time European Americans wanted or needed their land or its mineral content.

By the time the nation was established, slavery was firmly entrenched in the South, and racial prejudices pervaded the country on both sides of the Mason-Dixon line. Thus, the roots of oppression in racial prejudice against lower castes have a long-standing historical basis throughout the white community. In the early 19th century, Alexis de Tocqueville made a seemingly counterintuitive observation about prejudice and oppression in the United States: "The prejudice of race appears to be stronger in the states that have abolished slavery than in those where it still exists; and nowhere is it so intolerant as in those states where servitude has never been known" (quoted in Kovel, 1984, pp. 33-34). This statement becomes understandable only when we consider it in light of entitlement: Northern white abolitionists made Southern slaveholders painfully conscious of their racial prejudices and entitlement, but the Northerners failed to see their own.

By the time de Tocqueville made his observation, the differentiation between immigrant and caste minorities had become deeply ingrained in our national psyche. If African Americans or Native American Indians, as well as women, were to have any rights, those rights would not emerge organically as a natural outgrowth of social progress in a society that fully embraced these people as equal participants. Rather, vocal and often violent struggle was needed to extend the rights of citizenship to members of lower castes. Their strenuous efforts led to the passage of the Thirteenth (1865), Fourteenth (1868), and Fifteenth (1870) Amendments to the U.S. Constitution.

By the beginning of the 20th century, racists were hard-pressed to use their old justifications for their oppressive beliefs and actions. Thus, in place of the rantings of the early Christianizers, the perpetrators of racism pointed to Social Darwinism to rationalize their maintenance of racist institutions. Specifically, European American men perverted the work of Charles Darwin to suggest that they had all the power and all the privileges of society simply because they were the fittest to enjoy such power and privilege. The concept of Social Darwinism legitimized the power and privilege of a higher order of humans (i.e., themselves: white men).

Not everyone blithely accepted Social Darwinism, however. Determined suffragists forced men to pass the Nineteenth Amendment (1920) to the U.S. Constitution, which granted women the right to vote for the first time. Similarly, outspoken blacks formed the National Association for the Advancement of Colored People (NAACP) and started pressing for social justice through the legal system. Their efforts led to such changes as the *Brown v. Topeka Board of Education* (1954) decision.

Sadly, it has taken urban violence to prompt many of the changes that have benefited the lower castes. Throughout history and across the country, race riots have shown a consistent theme: People ultimately react violently to being denied basic human rights. After a particularly turbulent summer in the 1960s, President Lyndon Johnson appointed a special panel headed by former Illinois Governor Otto Kerner to determine the causes of urban unrest. Among the many remarkable features of the study, two stand out: (1) that it was written at all, and (2) that it was written by black and white moderates, not by wild-eyed radicals and fanatics (Terry, 1970). The Report of the National Advisory Commission on Civil Disorders (known as the Kerner Report; Riot Commission, 1968) identifies the causes of urban unrest as a white problem: "What white U.S. citizens never fully understand but what the Negro can never forget is that the white society is deeply implicated in the ghetto. White institutions created it, white institutions maintain it, and white society condones it" (p. 6).

The Kerner report was not the only outcome of angry and episodically violent reactions to oppression. Much legislation and many judicial decisions resulted that have extended civil rights to specific populations. This rich body of law that speaks to people's inalienable rights includes the Civil Rights Acts from 1866 to 1964, which have continually expanded the guarantees of citizenship to U.S. citizens who are not white landowning men; the U.S. Supreme Court decision of 1954 (*Brown v. Topeka Board of Education*), which struck down 16 states' antimiscegenation laws; and the Voting Rights Act of 1965, which made it realistic for African Americans to exercise their right to vote throughout the country. These hard-won liberties are still not guaranteed without ongoing efforts to preserve them, however. (Witness the abdication of affirmative action, both nationally and in many localities.)

Each of these historical and legal events has underlying moral issues. In each case, people identified a wrong and reacted angrily against it, often responding with legislative or judicial action. Perhaps surprisingly, the laws intended to right civil wrongs and inequities highlight the breadth and depth of entitlement: People have had to seek legal remedies to ensure the human rights of all cultural groups except wealthy white men. (This is not to deny that most laws, drafted and passed chiefly by middle- and upper-class white men, primarily benefit this empowered group, however.)

By the 1970s and 1980s, the preponderance of U.S. immigrants arrived from Pacific Rim, Latin American, and Asian countries. Now there are large groups of people of color, among which favorable and unfavorable distinguishing characteristics are made. Compounding the problem is the reality that many Latin American immigrants also have African or indigenous American backgrounds, and they may speak Spanish, Portuguese, or French as their native language. This multiethnicity blurs the issues of immigrant versus caste status for some groups. For instance, the caste and socioeconomic status of wealthy Hispanic (white) Cuban immigrants differs sharply from that of impoverished African (black) Cuban immigrants. Nonetheless, despite some blurring, the caste system is alive and well in contemporary America.

Caste Status and the Teaching of History

Prior to World War II, white males were the primary recipients of public and private education, and the version of history taught in schools reflected the views, beliefs, and interests of white males. To this day, most U.S. history textbooks fail to address the U.S. caste system or the distinction between caste and immigrant status. They also rarely mention the exclusivity of U.S. government, business, and educational enterprises. Oppressed U.S. citizens appear as single chapters, cursory comments, or footnotes, if they appear at all. The effect of this legacy of omission is an assumption of entitlement by members of dominant U.S. society, particularly white men. This dominant cultural perspective has thus been institutionalized in U.S. public schools. The effect on women has been to ensure their role as subordinate to men. The effect on people of color has been to ensure them of second-class citizenship and to deprive members of most cultural groups the education and access that would facilitate their success in the U.S. mainstream.

The unfortunate reality of most history textbooks is that they glorify the accomplishments of politicians, barons of industry, and warriors, but they spend comparatively little time on the social issues of each historical period. The accomplishments of white men are the major foci because government, business, and the military have been, and remain, the province of white men. When women and people of color have been recognized for their contributions to the development of our country, history textbooks have recorded their contributions as exceptions. This sends an insidious message to students about who is valued in this country.

The struggle for the rights of oppressed people predates the U.S. Revolutionary War, yet history textbooks have consistently failed to present the role of women and people of color in the development of the United States. For example, though urban violence has historical roots going back to the 18th century, the race riots of the 18th and 19th centuries are rarely recorded in modern U.S. history textbooks (Franklin & Moss, 1988). Hence, most U.S. citizens see urban race riots as an artifact of the modern civil rights movement. The view that urban violence is a recent phenomenon is further enhanced by modern media, which compete to provide the most sensational accounts of contemporary upheavals.

The Rolling Meadows consultants are presenting to Superintendent Watson's cabinet, and Holly, the assistant superintendent of curriculum and instruction, is not so sure they really understand the situation at Rolling Meadows because she hasn't seen any of these problems.

They say, "Throughout U.S. educational history, students have been taught little to nothing about the caste system in this country and precious little about U.S. citizens of lower castes. In recent decades, however, most textbooks and school curricula have inserted some materials and lessons mentioning women and people of color, although these insertions have generally been few and segregated from the sweep of U.S. history. Acknowledgment of African Americans is generally limited to scant lessons on slavery, the celebration of Dr. King's birthday, and observances of black history month in February. Lessons about Native American Indians often range from highlighting their nobility to underscoring their savagery; usually, their only significant role is to attend the first Thanksgiving. Lessons about Latinos are frequently relegated to music, dance, and a lesson about Cesar Chavez, if they are mentioned at all outside of the southwestern United States. Students learn about Asians as the celebrants of Chinese New Year, the sneaky attackers at Pearl Harbor, and the reluctant recipients of our 'help' during the Korean and Vietnam Wars. Lessons about women often resort to the great woman approach, focusing on a few heroic individuals rather than the historic and continuing role of women in the United States. These discrete lessons lead to the objectification and invisibility of girls and children of color."

These segregated lessons fail to teach students about how women and people of color have played vital roles throughout all aspects and periods of U.S. history. Lessons about a few isolated events and people cannot help students understand how such people and events relate to all U.S. history. Further, because the history of racism and other forms of oppression is absent from these lessons, most students (particularly white male students) fail to understand how current societal tensions have emerged from historical events and trends.

Although all students are kept ignorant of the history of women and people of color in U.S. life, white male students suffer the

least from this omission: They are still able to feel a connection to
their past. Their forebears appear on every page and in every
lecture. They are clearly a part of the U.S. pageant. In contrast,
students of color and female students feel disconnected from U.S.
history; none of their forebears appears to have been involved in
any significant way; people of color and women are largely
absent from the history being taught. As a result, students of color
and female students gain a sense of invisibility in our country's
history and literature due to the omissions, distortions, and fal-
lacious assumptions being taught in school.

White boys, never having this experience, have no idea how it
feels to be absent from history. Howard (1993) summarizes their
experiences well: "The possibility of remaining ignorant of other
cultures is a luxury uniquely available to members of any dominant group" (p. 38). This luxury extends to ignorance of the
oppression experienced by people of other cultures. This situation places a heavy burden on the culturally proficient educator.

Without an accurate historical perspective, both entitled and
oppressed people will continue to be intensely defensive and
protective when assessing contemporary and historical social
issues. People of color confront racism daily and are often exas-
perated by white people whose response to their frustrations
range from hostility to indifference based on profound ignorance.
For their part, white U.S. citizens who do not feel personally
responsible for racism, and men who do not understand their role
in perpetuating institutionalized sexism are frustrated by appar-
ently unsympathetic people of color and women. Consequently,
discussions of oppression and entitlement often lead to miscom-
munication and resentment. One side speaks from painful personal experience, whereas the other side perceives only appar-
ently inexplicable anger and personal attack. As a culturally
proficient educator, you can guide the teachers of history to be
more cognizant of the entitlement of some groups and more
proactive in ending oppression.

MANIFESTATIONS OF ENTITLEMENT

The teaching of history is just one way in which entitlement
is manifested. In this section, we discuss how entitlement is
manifested through the language used for describing oppressed

TABLE 5.2 Words Used to Describe Oppressed and Entitled Groups

Oppressed	Entitled
Inferior	Superior
Culturally deprived	Privileged
Culturally disadvantaged	Advantaged
Deficient	Normal
Different	Similar
Diverse	Uniform
Third world	First world
Minority	Majority
Underclass	Upper class
Poor	Middle class
Unskilled workers	Leaders

persons, the ways in which oppressed persons are objectified, and the differing access to power available to entitled persons versus oppressed persons.

The Language of Entitlement

To understand the empowered end of the entitlement continuum, we need to recognize how language dehumanizes people by objectifying them (making them objects). Historically, the dominant white male society has used demeaning terminology to focus social attention on groups with less power, implying that they are the cause of their own status as outsiders. Thus, language reflects the realities of power in this society. Educators are no strangers to uses of terminology that blames the victims for their oppression. Since the mid-1950s, educators have bombarded students, educational literature, and fellow professionals with terms attempting to explain the disparities between oppressed and entitled groups. Table 5.2 presents some of the more common terms.

Each of the terms in the left column in Table 5.2 describes groups that occupy the oppressed end of the entitlement continuum. The ideas represented by these terms are used to explain why students from these groups fail to perform at criterion levels. These terms serve two purposes: (1) Educators can use these terms to view each student, and the student's cultural group, as the source of any educational problem that arises; and (2) they narrow educators' focus so they disregard the group's environmental context (i.e., the institutionalized oppression to which members are subjected).

By using terms of oppression, we focus on what is wrong with the oppressed, thereby implying that they must be studied (to detect their specific flaws) and then fixed. The unquestioned use of these terms suggests that people of color, who are disproportionately represented on the oppressed end of the continuum, suffer from a pathological condition. At best, they are viewed as others (not us), and at worst, as deviants. This polarity of language and perceptions is reflected in the daily workings of schools. Notice that some labels have no comparable terms for the entitled groups—unless, of course, we wish to use *normal* or some other term signifying that white men are the standard against which other people are measured.

One of the consultants turns to a page on his flip chart with these quotations:
"If we are celebrating diversity, why don't we have celebrations like white history month?"

"The teacher wrote on my child's paper that she didn't understand the black inner-city experience. This child has never lived in the inner city! Her father is a chemist and I am a lawyer. Her teacher knows we are a middle-class family."

"These immigrant students don't even have magazines and books in their homes. They are at a tremendous disadvantage when compared to the other students."

After giving the cabinet members a chance to reflect on the effect of these statements, the consultant remarks, "Each of these comments assumes that entitled students are the standard of measure for other students. In the first comment, it is not recognized that most traditional school curricula celebrate the dominant culture daily. The second illustration shows the lack of awareness of the relationship of social class to ethnic culture. The last quote reflects the assumption that the speaker knows what is in students' homes and that the students with books and magazines read them!"

The terms in the right column in Table 5.2 describe the students representing the dominant culture of our country. Pause for a moment to consider this question: How often do you use these terms in your interactions with students and with fellow educators? Most of the people we ask answer not much or never. Most of us rarely utter these words because entitled people do not objectify or name themselves. Entitled people name only others, people they perceive to differ from themselves. Thus, when we use the terms *deficient* and *deprived* in their many permutations, we imply that entitled people are the norm by which we compare other people. We base that norm on white middle-class U.S. values and behaviors and, more specifically, on the values and behaviors of white middle-class men.

Labeling has trapped oppressed people in two ways: First, it confirms their status as outsiders to the dominant culture, ensuring that they will be denied access to societally valued cultural norms, and then it judges them deficient for failing to demonstrate these norms. The same thing goes for socioeconomic status: Oppressed people are denied access to the middle class, and then they are rebuked for failing to show middle-class values, attitudes, and behavior. In addition, they are denigrated not only as individuals who receive personalized oppressive labels but also as members of cultural groups that are castigated because of their likelihood to be given such labels.

Few entitled persons, however, can see the irony of these cultural and economic traps. As educators, we have to work hard to resist these labeling traps so that we can avoid referring to students and their families with multiple oppressive deficiency-based terms. As a culturally proficient educator, you can guide your colleagues in choosing terminology that affirms the value of each student, rather than focusing on how students deviate from the dominant culture.

Thingification: *The Face of the Enemy*

Kovel (1984) uses the term *thingification* to describe how members of dominant U.S. society use language to create distance between themselves and others. It gives the dominant group the power to establish, define, and differentiate outsiders as others. When we use such terms as *them* and *you people,* we objectify people. We manipulate people's self-perceptions and perceptions of others, while we reinforce a sense of otherness. Similarly, when we continue to use *man* and *he* as inclusive terms for women and men, we *thingify* women, placing women in the category of other (i.e., not men, the acknowledged norm).

Thingification is an extension of the institutionalized oppression never experienced by members of the dominant culture. It is part of a "matrix of culturally derived meanings" (Kovel, 1984, pp. 6-7) that allows the larger and empowered segment of society to communicate that minority groups are never quite as good as the dominant society. Is it surprising that oppressed people often react in a hostile manner to the use of these expressions?

The dominant culture conveys thingification by more means than just oppressive terminology. Consider the following news headline: "Whites Think Black Kids Can't Learn, Pollster Says," the title of an article reporting the findings of a Louis Harris Poll. Among other findings, the article reports that "up to 90% of respondents would support programs to break the cycle of poor, inner-city youngsters ending up on welfare." According to the report, "the view of 7 in 10 [respondents] is that if the U.S. does not properly educate its minorities and poor, then the U.S. will lose its competitive edge." It concludes that "the bottom line is that 37% of white America has written off black America as hopeless" (Association of California School Administrators, 1991). The article implies that the basic reason for educating children is to ensure the economic vitality of the nation.

The article on the poll (Association of California School Administrators, 1991) is an example of thingification. African American children are considered significant only to the extent that they can ensure U.S. economic self-sufficiency. If U.S. citizens could rely on a poorly educated labor force in this information age of the 21st century, as society did in the agricultural and industrial ages, we are led to believe that there would be no concern about the education of these children. The article is written with indifference toward the youths because neither educators nor society have given the education of African American or other nonwhite youths top priority. The reporter shows no moral outrage and makes no ethical comment regarding the observation that white America has written off black America.

Delpit (1988) describes the process of thingification in terms of how insiders (entitled persons) are viewed differently from outsiders (oppressed people). Specifically, insiders (i.e., heterosexual white men) are viewed as individuals with personal characteristics, but outsiders (i.e., people of color, women, and homosexuals) are viewed as representing their groups, such that their characteristics are deemed representative of their groups' characteristics. For instance, during job interviews, when a white male job applicant exhibits problems, he or she is judged to be a person with individual problems. When a person of color exhibits the same problems in an interview, the problem is assigned to the entire cultural group as a characteristic of that group.

This thingification of outsiders also applies to women and gay people. Men often discount the anger, annoyance, concerns, and health issues of women as insignificant characteristics of their hormonal cycles. When straight people observe a gay man or a lesbian frequenting a predominantly gay business, they assume that the person is doing something perverted or unsavory. When a straight man is angry, has a headache, or frequents an all-male business, however, he is considered to be behaving in ways that reflect on him as an individual, not on all men collectively.

Entitlement breeds thingification by making the humanity of thingified persons invisible. A person becomes invisible as an individual in many ways: by being viewed as unable to learn, by representing an entire group of people during an interview, or by having value only as a cog in the economic system. When whites perpetuate thingification and invisibility, incessantly view non-white groups negatively, and then refuse to acknowledge those realities, nonwhites often feel enraged (Ellison, 1952; Gilligan, 1983; Giroux, 1992; Kovel, 1984; Wright, 1940). The vast majority of white people, particularly white men, are astonished at this furor, however, because they have never experienced thingification. When confronted with this information, white men often respond by denying their individual participation in the process. They say, I identify myself as a person, not as a white man. Only the members of the dominant group are entitled to make such an assertion.

> Protestations to deny whiteness eliminate neither the fact nor the problem of white privilege. U.S. culture is color conscious. We sort people by color, to the advantage of some and detriment of others. To dissociate oneself from whiteness by affirming humanness ignores what whiteness has done and how we continue to benefit from it. (Terry, 1970, pp. 18-19)

Granted that straight white men have many pressures to perform, succeed, and survive, these pressures occur in a context absent of the additional and insupportable pressures of institutionalized oppression. As educators, we must understand these pressures, particularly if we belong to the dominant group in U.S. society. Such understanding is the foundation for creating a school system that addresses the needs of children as members of groups capable of learning, as opposed to being members of groups with deficiencies that limit their full participation in school or society.

Power

As mentioned in the discussion of U.S. history, the disenfranchised have had to seek legislative and judicial remedies to gain any power in this country, but wealthy white landowning men have assumed power from the very beginnings of U.S. history. Jacksonian democracy broadened the participation of U.S. citizens in the political and economic spheres of this country, but it denied such participation to anyone other than white men. U.S. white men have enjoyed power, as manifested in the form of privilege or entitlement, as an integral part of their history, tradition, and economic status.

The power that accrues to the entitled in our society is so pervasive that those who have it do not see the pervasiveness. This makes the goal of cultural proficiency difficult to achieve. In much the same way that people do not appreciate their liberties until they are threatened, most entitled white men do not appreciate the power of their entitlement because they have never experienced the absence of power. Moreover, the milieu of entitlement insulates them from hearing the cries of those who live in fear of sexual assaults, battering, racist acts, and other forms of discrimination or those who protest against the systematic denial of their access to societal power. Delpit (1988) notes two distinct responses to entitlement: (1) Those with greater power are frequently least aware of, or least willing to acknowledge, its existence; and (2) those with less power are often most aware of power discrepancies.

"What is at stake for white America today is not what [oppressed] people want and do but what white people stand for and do" (Terry, 1970, p. 15). Once all U.S. citizens understand and accept that some people receive entitlements based on gender and race, that other people have impediments placed before them for the same reason, and that all U.S. citizens have a responsibility to recognize that everyone is an integral part of both the problem and the solution, then true progress toward cultural proficiency can begin.

Recognizing Entitlement in Education

Since the late 1970s, we have involved thousands of educators, parents, and students in the simulation *Starpower* (Shirrts, 1969), which helps people notice the effects of entitlement and inequity.

In this simulation, participants create a three-tiered society where power and access are disproportionately distributed; they experience interactions within and among the groups in this simulated society; and then they debrief by discussing their feelings in their roles, as well as the applications of this experience to the real world.

In the simulation, one of the three groups is awarded the right to make the rules. The entitled group consistently makes rules that are to its advantage and that either overtly or covertly disadvantage the remaining two groups. In the debriefing discussion, those in the disadvantaged groups are incredulous that the rule makers do not see that they did not earn their power; rather, the society was organized to favor them.

Delpit's (1988) observation of educators debating issues related to educating children of color supports this notion of unawareness:

> For many who consider themselves members of liberal or radical camps, acknowledging personal power and admitting participation in the culture of power is extremely uncomfortable. On the other hand, those who are less powerful in any situation are most likely to recognize the power variable most acutely. My guess is that white colleagues . . . did not perceive themselves to have power over the nonwhite(s). . . . However, either by virtue of their position, their numbers, or their access to that particular code of power of calling upon research, the white educators had the authority to establish what was to be considered truth regardless of the opinions of people of color, and the latter were well aware of that fact. (pp. 283-284)

Given that most educational policymakers and decision makers are white men, this absence of information and insight becomes especially crucial to the culturally proficient leader. Many entitled members of society believe that all people in this country have the opportunity to succeed but choose instead to pick the scabs on old wounds so that they do not have to put forth effort in new endeavors. Entitlement creates either unawareness or denial of the reality that not all U.S. citizens have a common base of inalienable rights. These beliefs and denials are supported by curricula that are silent about the pluralistic nature of our country's history and development.

As a young teacher of social studies, even before going to Coolidge High School, Evan Brown was aware of being ill-prepared to provide for the black students in his classroom. To remedy that inadequacy, he enrolled in a degree program at a major midwestern university and took coursework on the history of the U.S. Negro. It did not take him long to identify the gaps in his undergraduate education. Moreover, he realized quickly that his white students would also benefit from this material, while at the same time he continued to puzzle many of his Euro-American professors and colleagues. They did not understand why a bright young white man with a fairly secure future would want to waste his time this way.

Evan also noticed the degree to which entitlement had affected his own perceptions. First, his prior education had provided almost no information on black history, thereby rendering it invisible, discounted entirely. Second, his original motivation to enroll in the courses, which had been to prepare himself to teach black students, changed with his realization that such information is of benefit to all students.

In 1968, he moved to California to continue his teaching career and to have two more startling experiences that increased his cultural proficiency. When he taught students of Mexican and Portuguese descent for the first time, he experienced the same sense of inadequacy he had felt in his midwestern classroom. Then, in discussing curricular content with colleagues, he was shocked to learn that U.S. citizens of Japanese ancestry had been incarcerated in U.S. relocation camps during World War II. His shock and anger were derived from two sources: (1) that his own country could do such a thing to its own citizens, and (2) that he had earned degrees in social studies from two reputable universities yet had no knowledge of this event.

The authors of history textbooks have routinely excluded some cultural groups from their writing; more insidiously, they have also excluded major events. When authors exclude this information from students' textbooks, they romanticize U.S. history, thereby failing to help young people understand many of the social conflicts that occur. Both the teaching of U.S. history and the outcomes of the simulation illustrate how entitlement is reinforced by experience.

Another illustration of how white men lack awareness of entitlement and deny its existence comes from the many sessions on cultural proficiency that we have conducted in recent years.

During an inservice session on cultural proficiency at the Coolidge District, Jim Woodard, the consultant, overhears this conversation between European American Principal Steve Petrossian and Puerto Rican Vice Principal Fernando Rios:

Steve says, "You know, this activity in determining how prejudice differs from racism or sexism gives me some new information. I had never considered the concept of power; it just never occurred to me. Let me ask you this, and you tell me what it is: One of my African American teachers said that one of our students is 'a good athlete for a white boy.' Now isn't that racism?"

"Steve," Fernando replies, "let me get this straight: You have been on this planet for decades, and you have never thought about the power that white people have in this country?"

Steve is defensive. "Hey, why attack me? I'm being straight with you. Power is something I've just never considered. Shoot, just because I'm white doesn't mean that I have power. Besides, you haven't answered my question. Isn't my story an example of racism?"

Jim responds to Steve. "No, it isn't. Although the story illustrates ethnocentric use of a stereotype, the teacher in your story lacks the power to institutionalize his or her belief."

Jim continues, addressing the whole group. "The story also shows Steve's lack of awareness of—and wish to deny—his own entitlement. The teacher in Steve's story was not reinforcing or perpetuating institutional racism, which affects every single person and has grave social consequences no matter whether it is recognized or acknowledged. More often than not, people who are not directly affected by oppression fail to understand when cultural groups speak out about their experiences. This failure is frequently translated into the egocentric view . . ."

Fernando interrupts: "Yeah, they say, 'If I didn't experience the oppression, or witness it, then you must be overreacting.' "

Jim continues, "If we are to create an effectively functioning society—and, by extension, a school system that is culturally proficient—we must find ways to address issues of entitlement. By doing so, we can minimize gaps in the education of our educators that perpetuate their lack of awareness and their denial of their own empowerment."

EDUCATIONAL PRACTICES OF ENTITLEMENT AND OPPRESSION

Unfortunately, the education system as we know it not only has failed to enlighten students and educators about oppression and entitlement but has further institutionalized the oppression of nondominant cultural groups by its very structure and operation. Two particularly egregious examples are systems of tracking and educator expectations.

Systems of Tracking

Oakes (1985), Oakes and Lipton (1990), and Wheelock (1992) have documented both the biases of entitlement built into the tracking system and its negative effects on students, as well as on society at large. Remember that in Chapter 3 in our discussion of leadership, tracking emerged during the late 19th and early 20th centuries, when educators were seeking ways to incorporate myriad European immigrants into the U.S. mainstream. The manifest function of tracking was to make the instructional system efficient, in accord with the then-current emphasis on the scientific management of schools. Today, we know that the latent—and perhaps often unintended—functions of tracking have been to harm students at the oppressed end of the entitlement continuum. Throughout the country, as schools move toward cultural proficiency, they are beginning to dismantle tracking systems and to focus on grouping systems that provide all students with equal access to information, skills, and values that foster success.

Even without a formal tracking system, however, U.S. students are tracked because of their color and the caste status that color imbues. The power of caste and entitlement is reflected in this playground rhyme:

If you're black, get back
If you're brown, stick around
If you're red, you're already dead
If you're yellow, you're mellow
If you're white, you're alright

Educator Expectations

Extensive research has shown that educators have differing expectations of students depending on the students' race, ethnicity, and gender. These studies have provided consistent data demonstrating stark disparities of class, caste, and entitlement in educators' interactions with students. Interactions based on poor expectations clearly lead to devastating consequences for students, in terms of both academic performance and self-image (Oakes, 1985; Oakes & Lipton, 1990; Rosenthal & Jacobsen, 1966; Wheelock, 1992).

As culturally proficient educators, we can strive to overcome these obstacles to learning through programs that provide models by which educators can learn of verbal and nonverbal behaviors that project the cultural expectation that all students can learn, thus providing them with equal opportunity in the classroom. Such programs can provide alternatives to perpetuating the judgments, expectations, and behaviors of entitled people blindly. Wheelock (1992) details scores of such programs that vary from hands-on approaches to conceptual papers. In this book, the activities selected for the Resources introduce concepts basic to understanding the cultural bases for expectations.

At Coolidge Middle School, this conversation takes place in the parking lot after a session with consultant Jim Woodard. Teacher DeLois says, "I am really enjoying this session on cultural proficiency. I can see where I can use a lot of this information to prepare the girls and Latinos in my classes better to assume a responsible role in society."

Dakota Blaine, the dean of discipline, lashes back, "Are you for real? I would like you and this 'cultural expert' to spend a day in my office. All I deal with is the scum of this school. If they were in your classroom, you would know why those people are so behind in school."

Ellie, another teacher, chimes in. "Let me tell you a thing or two. First, if you think the girls and the Mexicans are the ones who need help, you are in worse shape than you know. The true scum in this school are the professional educators who do not see students when they come to their office. All you see is the color of their skin, and you judge the kids and their families in the same way."

To deny either the overt or the covert presence of the attitudes reflected in this conversation is to be blind to the kinds of oppression to which unentitled children, particularly children of color, are subjected daily. We are not advocating color blindness. Rather, we urge culturally proficient educators to see what color means in the context of entitlement and oppression. Once educators see how they make judgments based on entitlement and oppression, they will recognize how such judgments influence their expectations and evaluations of students, the tracking of students, and the creation of instructional programs. Consider a discussion that takes place among some teachers at Coolidge High School.

"I have been at this school for 17 years, and have I seen some changes!" says Michelle.

"Like what?" Bobby queries.

"Well, first of all," Michelle responds, "when I first came here, this was a nice, stable, working-class community where the parents wanted their children to have more than they did. Sure we had problems, but nothing like today."

"Yeah," Lee joins in, "then 14 years ago, about the same time the forced busing started, the school became all black in no time at all!"

"And?" Bobby challenges.

"What do you mean, 'And'?" Lee is getting annoyed. "You know exactly 'and what.' That was when our test scores dropped, drug problems began, and the school became one more ghetto nightmare. And I'm not a racist, these are just facts!"

Michelle tries to clarify their position. "Of course we're not racist. At least now the demographics are on our side. With the Asian students we have now, parents see to it that their kids study, and the Latino kids, they keep their gang trouble out of the school and in their own neighborhoods."

A MORAL IMPERATIVE

Where should culturally proficient educators begin to attack tracking, educator expectations, and other manifestations of oppression? Cultural proficiency begins for white people with the awareness of the dynamics of entitlement. Although white men are particularly needful of gaining awareness, all successful public school educators have been indoctrinated in a system that perpetuates racism, sexism, and other forms of oppression. All educators pass through this system as they prepare to transmit the values and the culture of the dominant society to public school children. This preparation is couched in such terms as *responsible citizenship* and *civics*. In reality, through this system, educators learn to prepare students to sustain the status quo and to maintain and support U.S. democratic society as it exists today. Educators might risk being accused of treason or labeled as anarchists if they were to teach students to challenge societal norms overtly, to accept lifestyles and values considered deviant by middle America, or to advocate for societal change. Public schools were not designed to stimulate controversy, and public school educators are not expected to teach students to question, let alone defy, authority.

Culturally proficient leaders understand this process and are aware of the subtle ways entitlement and oppression are fostered. They understand that educators have furthered the programs and practices that have served to enhance opportunities for some people while denying access to those opportunities for others, whether intentionally or unwittingly. They encourage fellow educators to recognize that a student's native culture and values are important for the student's survival in his or her family and community. They encourage teachers to complement their native values with an understanding of the values of dominant U.S. society. At the same time, culturally proficient leaders work with colleagues to challenge some of the assumptions of dominant U.S. values and to raise the dynamics of entitlement to a conscious level.

Oddly, U.S. educators have spent much energy studying the phenomena of African American underachievement, the needs of Mexican American students, why girls do not take mathematics, and the perceived deviance of homosexuals, but have spent little or no energy studying the context within which all students perform. Professionals from all fields have debated the success of school, the failure of school, the deschooling of the society, and the reasons for each. They have used private and public funds to document, study, and recommend. Yet the situation continues and does not appear to improve. In fact, it is regressing for African American and Latino males. The problem in education has been studied from every conceivable angle—except where the problem lies: The problem lies in the United States' failure to make a moral commitment to provide education for all groups of society. By making this moral commitment, we can break this country's last tie with its apartheid-based history and we may find the means for creating an authentic culturally proficient future.

Despite the historical and legal data pointing to the need, we educators have yet to make a moral commitment to confronting entitlement and eliminating oppression. To do so, we must look at schools in the context of a society governed by class, caste, and entitlement, and we must examine the role schools play in inculcating and endorsing the values of dominant society. To do that, we must abandon the notion that there is something wrong with people because of their racial, ethnic, or gender membership. We must examine in depth the barriers placed in people's paths, then we must recognize our own responsibility to begin tearing down the barriers constructed by straight white men and other entitled people.

As culturally proficient educators, when we begin to raise our own level of consciousness about the dynamics of oppression, we usually begin with an aspect of oppression that more directly affects us. For instance, Peggy McIntosh (1988) recalls her experiences with this personal growth:

> After I realized, through faculty development work in women's studies, the extent to which men work from a base of unacknowledged privilege, I understood that much of their oppressiveness was unconscious. Then I remembered the frequent charges from women of color that white women whom they encounter are oppressive. I began to understand why we are justly seen as oppressive, even when we don't see ourselves that way. At the very least, obliviousness of one's privileged state can make a person or group irritating to be with. (p. 4)

McIntosh's (1988) experience of learning about the bases of sexism led her to an examination of privilege, then dominance, then power. When she attained higher levels of awareness, she was able to look around herself and see that issues of power included racism and heterosexism as well as sexism. McIntosh then questioned the desirability of her own privilege gained through this process, noting that it can lead to moral weakness in those who depend on it. It is imperative that white men and other entitled persons assume this responsibility for consciousness raising. In addition to raising our own consciousness, investigation of one's own prejudices and entitlements enables us both to serve as role models against prejudice and to implement culturally proficient leadership practices (Pate, 1988).

As culturally proficient educators, we must interpret our discomfort with these issues as a sign of where we need to begin becoming more aware of our own entitlement. Often, when we discuss, debate, and argue about the manifestations of oppression identified in this book, deep and intense emotions erupt. On the one hand, people who are targets of oppression often feel angry and frustrated with their day-to-day experiences. On the other hand, people who have never experienced these forms of oppression often feel guilty or defensively angry at being held responsible for things they never intentionally created. That anger, in turn, feeds the frustration of those who are victimized, for they cannot believe the naïveté of the dominant groups, and the spiral of ire winds ever higher.

To develop our own consciousness and to be effective as culturally proficient leaders, we must view our own group membership within a realistic context of entitlement and oppression. In his work with counselor educators, Ponterotto (1988) has developed a stage model of racial consciousness that readily applies to all educators. (See Table 5.3, which describes each stage and shows how Pontoretto's model compares with the cultural proficiency curriculum.) Ponterotto is careful to note that not all people reach the fourth stage. When expanding the self-examination to include issues of race, ethnicity, and gender, it seems even less likely that all people will reach the fourth stage. Our inability to achieve perfection, however, should not deter attempts to strive for greater proficiency. It is our collective responsibility to keep the issues of cultural proficiency out in the open so we can make steady progress in serving the needs of all students. Such an approach is more ethical and morally responsible because it shifts us away from blaming the victim to seeking constructive ways to educate all people.

The development of moral character and strength has long been an important cornerstone of public and private education. When we build on this foundation an examination of privilege, domination, and power as central to the understanding of prejudice and oppression, we construct a stronger edifice of education. To serve the needs of all youths, educators must clearly recognize that we now distribute social privileges inequitably, providing them freely to some students and rationing them meagerly to others. This may be more important to understand for those who are most entitled (i.e., white men) than it is for any other sector of society. In the same way that students from oppressed groups need role models, white and male students need role models to help them learn about unearned, unconscious privilege. Once they begin to acknowledge their entitlement, they will be better prepared to take a responsible role in the cultural proficiency continuum.

Various educational practices have been developed and studied that, when used by educators who understand the oppression-entitlement continuum, result in positive educational experiences for students regardless of their social status. Many researchers (e.g., Comer, 1988; Levin, 1988; Sadker & Sadker,

TABLE 5.3 Stages of Racial Consciousness

Stage	Comparable Place on the Cultural Proficiency Continuum	Description
Stage 1: Preexposure	Cultural destructiveness or cultural incapacity	People have given little thought to multicultural issues or to their role in a racist and oppressive society
Stage 2: Exposure	Cultural incapacity	People are confronted with the realities of racism and prejudice, and they examine their own cultural values and may feel guilt or anger
Stage 3: Defensive	Cultural blindness	People retreat from the issues altogether
Stage 3: Zealot	Cultural precompetence	People zealously or defensively take on the minority plight
Stage 4: Integration	Cultural competence and cultural proficiency	The zealousness of the previous stage becomes more balanced in multicultural interests or endeavors, and the defensiveness lessens because the airing of feelings gives way to interest in, respect for, and appreciation of cultural differences

Adapted from Ponterotto (1988), pp. 151-153.

1994; Sizer, 1985) have demonstrated that all children are capable of excelling in all areas of schooling. Culturally proficient leaders must value the diversity present in the school setting and then take steps to evaluate the culture of the school and its educators by clarifying values, assumptions, and cultural expectations. They must learn about the cultures of the students and their families and assess the dynamic nature of the differences in values and expectations. Cummins (1988) and Sleeter (1991) have observed that

> empowering education programs work with students and their home communities to build on what they bring; disabling programs ignore and attempt to eradicate knowledge

and the strengths students bring, and replace them with those of the dominant society. (Sleeter, 1991, p. 5)

Culturally proficient leaders work with their colleagues to adapt the school program so it addresses the needs of all students, not just the entitled ones.

❧ SIX ❧

Moving Toward Cultural Proficiency

In fewer than 10 years, Rolling Meadows has changed from almost totally white to majority Cuban (most of whom are first generation immigrants) with Armenian, Korean, and white students having comparable numbers. After several years of declining test scores, rapid student growth (from 1,000 to 2,000 students; partly from growth but also from the addition of the ninth grade), and increasing student-to-student conflicts, the principal of several years was forced into retirement. This very insular district rarely hired administrators from outside, but in this case, it went outside the district and hired the district's first woman, Julie Scales, who is also the first African American high school principal. She has served as an assistant principal in another state, but this is her first principalship. In her first 2 years, there was little evidence that anyone mentored her or showed her the "Rolling Meadows way of doing business." Another pressure on Julie is that last year the school was given a partial, temporary accreditation from the regional accrediting agency (rather than the full accreditation), which was a blow to the egos in the district and the community.

It was only after a consultant spent 6 days on campus interviewing teachers, students, aides, administrators, and parents and issued a report of her findings that the district administrators examined the fact that the mission of the school had changed. It had been a school that "prepared students for college"; now it is a school that also has to prepare students to become citizens of this country.

As educators and organizational development consultants, we have been providing training in what is now called diversity training since the days of confrontational sensitivity training. During the conversations that led to writing this book, we concluded that reflecting on our past and what we have learned from our clients could be important to others who wish to contribute to peace, justice, and harmony in their communities. Collectively, we have more than 75 years as consultants, many of which have been filled with great frustration because we know that no matter how hard we try, many in our audiences will remain hostile and will change only as a result of court orders or mandates from the hierarchical leaders in the district. Our early years as diversity trainers were frustrating because as we felt unsuccessful, we could see that many of the children and teachers with whom we worked were unsuccessful. Teachers were not reaching children, children were not reaching minimal standards, and educational leaders were not reaching out to their colleagues or their communities in meaningful ways. When we reviewed the effectiveness of the various types of human relations and diversity training, we found, at best, mixed results ranging from major changes in attitudes and behaviors for some individuals to relatively minor change for most schools and districts.

Laws have been passed and policies have been established that have lowered many of the societal barriers to access, particularly in the areas of race and gender equity. There are still very broad gaps between the perception of what is needed and the activity taken to achieve those goals, however. U.S. citizens could have the same experience and have opposing views based on their previous cultural experiences about what it means. These disparate opinions range from welfare for immigrants to basic rights for gay men and lesbians. Then we stumbled upon Terry Cross's (Cross et al., 1989) model of cultural competence.

In a workshop for California staff analysts, one of the participants mentioned that a less-than-sensitive comment made by one of her colleagues was "not culturally competent." After a few questions and a visit to her office at lunchtime, we had in our hands *Toward a Culturally Competent System of Care* (Cross et al., 1989). It was directed toward mental health workers and had been written in response to a situation where Native American Indian families were labeled as pathologically dysfunctional because they did not meet the norms the middle-class European American clinicians were using to assess the health of a family.

We immediately saw the relevance of cultural competence to every organization we had ever worked with. We had spent most

The university is dedicated to learning, teaching, and serving society through education, research, and public service. Our international reputation for excellence is due in large part to the cooperative and entrepreneurial nature of the university community. University faculty, staff, and students are encouraged to be creative and are rewarded for individual as well as collaborative achievements.

To foster the best possible working and learning environment, the university strives to maintain a climate of fairness, cooperation, and professionalism. These principles of community are vital to the success of the university and the well-being of its constituents. University faculty, staff, and students are expected to practice these basic principles as individuals and in groups.

Valuing Diversity

- We value the cultural diversity of the university because it enriches our lives and the university. We celebrate the diversity and support respect for all cultures, by both individuals and the university as a whole.

- We represent diverse races, creeds, cultures, and social affiliations coming together for the good of the university and those communities we serve. By working together as members of the university community, we can enhance the excellence of our institution.

Assessing One's Culture

- We value each member of the university community for his or her individual and unique talents, and applaud all efforts to enhance the quality of campus life. We recognize that each individual's effort is vital to achieving the goals of the university.

- We reject acts of discrimination based on race, ethnicity, gender, age, disability, sexual orientation, religion, and political beliefs, and we will confront and appropriately respond to such acts.

Managing the Dynamics of Difference

- We affirm each individual's right to dignity and strive to maintain a climate of justice marked by mutual respect for each other.

- We acknowledge that our society carries historical and diverse biases based on race, ethnicity, gender, age, disability, sexual orientation, religion, and political beliefs. Therefore, we seek to foster understanding and tolerance among individuals and groups, and we promote awareness through education and constructive strategies for resolving conflict.

Figure 6.1. Essential Elements of Cultural Proficiency and University Principles of Community

---

Institutionalizing of Cultural Knowledge

- We affirm the right to freedom of expression at the university. We promote open expression of our individuality and our diversity within the bounds of courtesy, sensitivity, confidentiality, and respect.

- We are committed to the highest standards of civility and decency toward all. We are committed to promoting and supporting a community where all people can work and learn together in an atmosphere free of abusive or demeaning treatment.

Adapting to Diversity

- We are a university that adapts responsibly to cultural differences among the faculty, staff, students, and community.

- We are committed to the enforcement of policies that promote the fulfillment of these policies.

Figure 6.1. *(Continued)*

of our careers working in thousands of organizations—schools, businesses, and not-for-profit agencies—that had values that were not culturally competent. We recognized how easily this concept could be adapted to educational settings as well as to other organizations. We also saw what we had missed in our years as frustrated diversity consultants.

We had approached our work from the perspective of first changing attitudes and then expecting the attitudes to result in behavioral changes. We knew that a values-based approach is doomed to fail in environments where people are forced to make change. We also knew that any approach to diversity that is perceived as "added on" as opposed to something that is "integral to" the core curriculum is doomed as well. Cultural competence is a behaviorally based approach to diversity. It does not depend on "right values" to work. Cultural competence is an approach that is easily integrated into the culture of the organization that adopts it. For that very reason, cultural competence looks different in every organization. It becomes a part of the organization's culture. Even in the field of education, one culturally competent school could look quite different from another culturally competent school. Figure 6.1 shows how one of our clients, a university, developed a code of behavior that describes in terms meaningful to that community the essential elements of cultural competence.

After our first few workshops, which we called "Moving Toward Cultural Competence," our participants told us that if we really wanted to get their attention, we had to change the title. Most people, especially people of color, feel they are already culturally competent. So we raised the stakes. "Come learn to be culturally proficient," we invited them. And they came. Over the past 10 years, we have introduced the cultural proficiency model to schools throughout California and to many organizations across the country. One of our clients has made a total commitment to cultural proficiency. A hospital we have been working with for 3 years has trained all 2,500 managers, staff, and doctors in the concept. It has incorporated the essential elements into its core competencies used for performance appraisal and related the essential elements to the core values of the hospital, which are printed on the ID badges that staff wear every day. Table 6.1 provides examples of the behavioral competencies the hospital wrote for each element of cultural proficiency.

When we began work at the hospital, the executive managers and the human resources team of the hospital (comparable to the administrators and staff development specialists of a school) demanded in-depth training in cultural proficiency because they knew they had to provide the day-to-day coaching, support, and reinforcement. They told us, "If we are going to walk the talk, we need to know not only what we are supposed to do, we need to know how, and we need to practice together." This hospital also has an in-house team of diversity trainers who we trained. After working with us, these trainers developed a training module that they delivered during the first round of training for all employees. We are now devising a plan for Phase II Intervention. We expect there will be more training, more work with the formal and nonformal leaders of the organization, more resistance from the staff, and more growth for the organization.

Educators are always trying something new, and the education process changes very slowly. Unfortunately, because of this pattern, the educators we encounter are either profoundly impressed with cultural proficiency or fundamentally weary of all they have to do to get through a school day without one more thing added to their agenda. Or they are both. The point we would like to emphasize is that cultural proficiency is not an add-on program. It is an inside-out approach to addressing the issues of diversity in a classroom, school, and district. It is an approach that is to be integrated into the culture of the school.

In reading the case study, you perhaps noticed that both Rolling Meadows and Coolidge started slowly and continued to enlarge and enhance the changes made as they worked toward becoming culturally proficient. Movement toward cultural proficiency usually begins with one or two people. We like to think of our sphere of influence as a pebble dropped in a pond. All of us get at least one pebble. We can choose to hold on to it and put it away in our pockets, or we can use it in some way. You can drop your pebble into a small puddle and make a big splash; you can toss it into a large lake and make almost no perceptible difference. Or you can join with a few others and together toss your pebbles into the same place and create a rippling effect that affects everything on the surface and profoundly affects those areas on which the pebbles fall.

How the members of a school or district use their influence is related to the leadership that exists there. Many books on organizational development and leadership explicate the concepts we summarize in Chapter 3. We want to emphasize two things:

1. You don't have to have a title to be a leader.

2. Research on leadership, organizations, and change does not have to be written specifically for schools for it to be useful.

Change takes place because people are open and ready for something new. They are able to look around and see a future that is different and better. They are able to rally their colleagues around this vision and work together to make it a reality. This takes place one step at a time, one classroom at a time, one school at a time, one pebble at a time. The first commitment must be to trust the process. Understand that it will take time and keep working at it until you begin to see changes in the attitudes and behaviors of your colleagues and coworkers. There is a tendency to stop or change programs when the agreed-on processes meet resistance. This is unfortunate, because resistance is a natural and expected step in the change process.

So where do you start? Start with where you are. Use the cultural proficiency continuum (Figure 2.2) to assess situations that have taken place in your school. Use the human relations needs assessment (Activity 3.5) to get a pulse of your district. If

TABLE 6.1 Performance Competencies and the Essential Elements of Cultural Proficiency

Key Tasks	Essential Elements and Units of Competence

■ Aware of and respects culturally diverse work environment; cares about customers, team members, and colleagues
■ Celebrates the success of the work team and of individuals within it
■ Reflects understanding that we come together in a common purpose and sees how much stronger and successful we are as a team
■ Demonstrates understanding of the Medical Center's vision
■ Actively participates on team committees
■ Participates in hiring new team members
■ Inspires a shared vision
■ Makes recommendations so that a sufficient number of qualified and competent persons provide care and services
	■ **Values Diversity**
	  ■ Finds reasons to compliment the strengths of staff and colleagues
	  ■ Reviews patient surveys to devise plans for addressing patient needs

■ Provides orientation to unit that includes description of the culture and the unwritten rules	■ **Assesses Culture** ■ Continually checks to learn staff assumptions about what is expected, based on understanding of unwritten rules

■ Demonstrates commitment to clear and regular communication to support coworkers and leadership
■ Conducts self in professional and ethical manner
■ Determines the qualifications and competence of department/service staff who provide care or services
■ Provides counseling to staff with continuing performance problems
■ Maintains an atmosphere of openness, honesty, and trust
■ Consistently pursues progress, applying critical thinking, problem solving, and follow-through
	■ **Manages the Dynamics of Difference**
	  ■ Demonstrates effective strategies for conflict management
	  ■ Acknowledges own mistakes

TABLE 6.1 *Continued*

Key Tasks	Essential Elements and Units of Competence
■ Encourages others to be self-directed learners, to try new ideas, and to measure and recognize results ■ Models behavior consistent with the core values ■ Assists team members in learning new skills ■ Assists team members in refining a skill they have ■ Orients, trains, and continually educates all persons within the department/service ■ Coaches teams on interpersonal skills and how to deal with conflict	■ **Institutionalizes Cultural Knowledge** ■ Creates environment in which team members are comfortable, explaining culturally specific behaviors to one another ■ Includes expectations for cultural competence in all training
■ Applies appropriate policy and procedure ■ Develops and implements policies and procedures that guide and support the provision of services ■ Serves as a catalyst toward change ■ Demonstrates ability to work well in a changing environment	■ **Adapts to Diversity** ■ Conducts ongoing review of policies and practices for unintentional discrimination

you have core values or a mission statement for the district, see which parts you can connect to the guiding principles of cultural proficiency (Figure 2.4). At a staff development meeting, conduct the shared values activity (Activity 6.2) to get a collective commitment to addressing the issues of diversity.

Once you have gathered these data, you are ready to examine the school or district through different lenses.

- ■ The continuum data provide you with a perspective on how you and others view the school. You may find widely different points of view on where the school or district is placed on the continuum. Sharing your views and earnestly listening to the views of others is an important initial step in developing shared meaning about how people experience the school or district.

- The needs assessment data provide even more detailed information on how different groups experience the school or district. When analyzed along with the impressionistic data of assessing where the school lies on the cultural proficiency continuum, powerful images begin to emerge. You get a picture of why some groups are happy with the school and why other groups may not be as content.
- Now you are ready to analyze your school or district's core values or mission statement. As you can imagine, at this point in the analysis process, you begin to see how data about the school and its needs are aligned with the core values and mission statement.
- At this point, your group is well prepared to do the shared values activity. This activity has the group commit to a culturally proficient environment by embracing values that support students' access to learning.

What you have created with these activities is agreement to examine schools through a different lens. The new lens frames new assumptions about access, oppression, and entitlement. This new lens is based in the acknowledgement of the reality of these social phenomena; it moves beyond the angst of guilt and anger to taking responsibility for schools being effective in the education of all students. It moves school leaders away from explaining why groups of students fail, toward determining what school leaders do to create powerful teaching-learning environments that ensure student success. This new lens allows educators to recognize and respond to both individual and group differences.

This book is more about beginnings than endings. With the concepts presented and the activities and cases provided, you now have the tools for taking the responsibility to begin the process of creating a culturally proficient school.

Let Us Hear From You

Once you have started to advance the cause of cultural proficiency, let us hear from you. Let us know what you are doing and how it is going for you. Tell us how this book has been useful and what additional resources you think you need. As you work with the concepts of cultural proficiency and develop substantive process for reinforcing the concepts, send us descriptions and tell us about the arenas in which you are working. Send us copies of the materials you develop as you integrate the concepts of cultural proficiency into your school or district culture. We will include those activities in subsequent editions of this book.

> Randall B. Lindsey, PhD; Kikanza Nuri Robins, EdD;
> Raymond D. Terrell, EdD
> The Cultural Proficiency Group
> 5600 San Marino Way
> Rancho Cucamonga, CA 91739
> (909) 899-0657

Structured Activities for Developing Culturally Proficient Leaders

We have used the activities in this Resource section as we have helped schools and other organizations move toward cultural proficiency. The activities are not designed to make changes in and of themselves, nor are they designed to be used as the only intervention in a diversity program. They are designed to be used as part of a comprehensive plan for approaching diversity issues in your school or district. Some of these activities will help you build trust among the members of the planning group. Others will help you introduce and reinforce the guiding principles and essential elements of cultural proficiency. The remainder of the activities will help you explore the concepts that we have presented in the book, or they will help you facilitate the planning necessary to embrace the cultural proficiency approach as a school or district. We have organized the activities to correspond with the concepts presented in each chapter. There is no one right order for facilitating the activities. Make your decisions based on the skill of the facilitator and the maturity of the group. Never conduct an activity simply as a space filler. Always relate the activity to something that the participants already know and to concepts you want to reinforce.

Before you get started, we recommend two activities using the materials in Figures R.1 and R.2. Each invites you to reflect on your role as a culturally proficient facilitator and trainer. Take the time yourself or with your training team to explore and discuss each point. Discuss ways that you have or can reflect your understanding of each suggestion in the work that you do. With Figure R.2, you may want to facilitate a conversation wherein the group writes a similar list for culturally proficient elementary/secondary teachers or administrators. Figure 2.3 may also be a useful tool in that process.

With so many great activities for getting people to think about issues of diversity and to reflect on their own developing cultural competence, you may be tempted to skip the text and to proceed to these activities. We do not recommend that. First of all, these activities are directly linked to the text and the portion of the case study found in each chapter. Reading the text and discussing the case study will provide a context for these activities. Second, before conducting an activity, it is very important to assess the readiness of the group and the expertise of the facilitator in working with groups on issues of diversity.

Readiness is determined by the experience the group members have in

- Effectively responding to conflict situations
- Openly discussing difficult issues
- Honestly articulating their feelings
- Comfortably interacting to people who strongly disagree with them
- Willingly examining their own values and behavior
- Candidly examining the school's policies, procedures, and practices for benign discrimination

The expertise of facilitators is determined by

- The amount of time and variety of experiences they have had facilitating both hostile and friendly groups as they address issues of diversity
- Their sensitivity to the dynamics of group process

14 Ways for Facilitators to Communicate That They Care

These behaviors have been proven in studies since the turn of the century to communicate to students, employees, and participants in workshops that the facilitator values the individuals and expects high achievement from them. Consistent use of these behaviors will result in better performance from the people in your group. These behaviors facilitate harmonious and productive behavior.

1. **Proximity:** Arrange the furniture in a way that acknowledges the contributions of the group rather than focusing all the attention on you. Move around so that everyone feels that they have access to you.

2. **Courtesy:** Use courteous words frequently and equitably with all participants. Model courteous behavior between you and the group and insist on courtesy among them.

3. **Accept feelings:** Acknowledge and accept feelings in a nonjudgmental manner. Everyone in the group is not going to be happy to be there. It is all right for people not to feel excited about you or the task. There are, however, appropriate ways of expressing unhappiness. Make those boundaries clear when it is necessary.

4. **Personal interest:** Ask questions or make statements relating to outside activities of the group members, their interests, and their experiences. Acknowledge that they have lives and interests outside of the work you are currently doing. Share interests that you have in common with the people in your group.

5. **Listening:** Listen attentively and empathetically to everyone. Convey to the group members that their feelings are understood and accepted. Acknowledge the contributions each person makes to discussions, linking their points to the subject being discussed.

6. **Equal distribution of response opportunity:** Provide an opportunity for everyone to respond to questions, express opinions, give reports, or participate in task-related discussions. The response should be public, the opportunity should be directed to the group member, and the response should be acknowledged by you.

7. **Latency:** Allow each group member a minimum of 5 seconds to think questions over before terminating the response opportunity or attempting to assist the person. Do not interrupt thinking time.

8. **Delving:** Provide additional information and cues to help people respond to questions. Rephrase questions or ask simpler questions that will lead to the current question. Provide clues or ask different but related questions.

9. **Higher-level questioning:** Ask people to express their opinions about the information, to evaluate it, to discover connections between several bits of information, to suggest how or why, or to organize information.

10. **Praise performance:** Inform staff who perform well that their performance is acceptable. Be clear and direct; tailor your responses to individual staff members and their specific job performance.

Figure R.1. Handout Sample

11. **Reason for praise:** Say exactly why you are praising people. Be specific so that the appropriate response or behavior can become a part of the person's ongoing effective performance and will be understood by the others as behavior worthy of praise.

12. **Individual help:** During the initial stages of a new assignment or project, make yourself available to provide help on an individual basis. Everyone will not need it, but each person should feel he or she can get direction and assistance if necessary.

13. **Touching:** Touching people during the course of communication is natural and desirable for most people. Studies reveal that human touch can mean the difference between life and death for infants and senior citizens. If you are a toucher and are sensitive to not violating the boundaries of those who do not want to be touched, touching people can be a very effective tool. Be sure to touch (not caress or fondle) in "neutral" areas (the area of the shoulder that would be covered by a shoulder pad; the forearm between the wrist and elbow) in a nonsexual way.

14. **Desisting:** Develop fair and consistent methods for stopping undesirable or socially unacceptable behavior without escalating anxieties or hostilities or causing further disruption.

Thanks to Patricia Schmuck, Sam Kerman, Mary Martin, Elsa Brizzi, and Dolores Grayson for their inspiration and their work in teacher expectations.

Figure R.1. *(Continued)*

- The work they have done on their own issues related to diversity
- The experience they have had working with hostile or reticent groups
- The skills they have in focusing and supporting groups ready for change
- Their recognition that debriefing is the most important part of a structured activity
- The skills they have for eliciting and integrating insights and conclusions during debriefing sessions

We have coded each activity so that you can see the minimum level of experience and readiness we recommend for the activity to be successful. In the example below, the activity requires an extensive degree of facilitator experience and an intermediate level of group readiness.

The Culturally Proficient Trainer

1. **Values diversity:** Is glad for the challenges diversity brings to the training room and overtly acts to diversify the training group.

2. **Assesses culture:** Is aware of his or her own culture and the effect it may have on people in the classroom. Asks for information about the culture of the organization and the cultures reflected in the demographics of the participants, and prepares for them.

3. **Manages the dynamics of difference:** Uses inclusive language, challenges and offers alternatives to the inappropriate or culturally blind language of others. Understands that what appears to be personality clashes may be clashes in gender, generation, or culture. Builds conflict resolution skills for desisting, mediating, interpreting, and explaining the conflicts caused by differences, and incorporates those skills in the facilitating of training sessions.

4. **Institutionalizes cultural knowledge:** Takes advantage of teachable moments to impart information about others. Provides language and perspectives to participants to help them ask questions, rather than making judgments, acting on assumptions, or responding to stereotypes.

5. **Adapts to diversity:** Reads, discusses, asks for feedback. Cultivates relationships with people of other cultures who can share their knowledge and understanding. Continually improves by changing presentation and facilitation techniques as he or she integrates new knowledge and understanding into work.

Figure R.2. Handout Sample

		Expertise of Facilitator		
		Low	*Moderate*	*Extensive*
Readiness of Group	Beginning			
	Intermediate			X
	Advanced			

If you would like to develop your skills as a facilitator, consider taking a course in training for trainers from the American Society for Training and Development (703-683-8100) or a course that will help you process your own diversity issues from the National Training Labs (207-824-2151).

❖RESOURCE A: Activities for Chapter 2❖

ACTIVITY 2.1: WHO AM I?

This activity introduces concepts basic to Chapter 2 by building an appreciation of how people identify themselves.

		Expertise of Facilitator		
		Low	*Moderate*	*Extensive*
Readiness of Group	Beginning	X		
	Intermediate			
	Advanced			

Purpose

To serve as a get-acquainted activity and to understand how others name themselves

Time Needed

45 minutes

Materials

- Chart paper
- Markers
- Paper and pencils for participants

Briefing

This activity will give you a chance to hear how others in your group define themselves and understand the relative importance of culture and ethnicity.

Process

1. As a group, develop a list of adjectives that describe the roles and groups with which the people in the group identify. Complete the sentence stem: "I am a(n) . . ." For example, "I am a(n) . . .

   African American"

   woman"

educator"

college graduate"

teacher"

administrator"

European American"

Hispanic American"

Asian Pacific Islander"

husband"

significant other"

partner"

gay man"

lesbian"

daughter"

brother"

2. Everyone takes the list of adjectives and ranks them individually, according to how they define themselves, omitting adjectives that do not apply.

Debriefing

1. What criteria did you use to rank the descriptors?

2. What surprised you about your list?

3. What surprised you about the list of the other members in your small group?

4. What have you learned about the members of this group?

5. What have you learned about labels, descriptors, and naming oneself?

6. How will you use this information?

ACTIVITY 2.2: TOTEMS—GETTING TO KNOW YOU

This is a useful activity for introducing the concept of culture as discussed in Chapter 2. Through using the concepts in Step 2 of the process, you can introduce the concept of culture in a safe and nonthreatening manner. By using the suggestions in the Variation section, you can get to a deeper understanding of culture and how people react to difference.

		Expertise of Facilitator		
		Low	*Moderate*	*Extensive*
Readiness of Group	Beginning	X		
	Intermediate			
	Advanced			

Purpose

To help members of the group get to know one another in terms of cultural similarities and differences

Time Needed

30 minutes

Materials

- Copies of blank totems, coats of arm, or large circles on 8½ × 11 paper
- Masking tape
- Colored markers

Briefing

We are going to engage in an activity so that you can get to know one another better and to understand the diversity of your backgrounds.

Process

1. Distribute blank sheets. Allow participants to select the form they wish to use.

2. Ask participants to draw symbols on their papers to represent
   a. Where they were born
   b. A strong family value
   c. Their present occupation
   d. A dream or fantasy
   e. A personal goal for this program
3. Tape paper to each person's chest and walk around the room looking at the drawings of the other participants, asking questions as appropriate.

Debriefing

1. What did you see that surprised you?
2. What did you learn about your colleagues?
3. What did you learn about yourself?
4. What conclusions can we draw about the members of this group?

Variation

Change the theme from getting to know you to diversity or some other topic by changing the symbols you ask participants to draw. For example:

1. The group with which they most strongly identify
2. How they are like the members of that group
3. How they do not fit a stereotype of that group
4. An event when they felt very different
5. A person who has most influenced them in understanding or accepting diversity

ACTIVITY 2.3: INTRODUCTORY GRID

This is a very good "sponge" activity that orients participants to the differences and similarities of the people in the room. (As an opener or closer, it soaks up extra people and extra time. People do not have to start at the same time to benefit from the activity.)

		Expertise of Facilitator		
		Low	*Moderate*	*Extensive*
Readiness of Group	Beginning		X	
	Intermediate			
	Advanced			

Purpose

To help people get acquainted with each other

Time Needed

Because this is a sponge activity to be used at the beginning of a session, 10-20 minutes for the activity and the debriefing is sufficient.

Materials

- Chart paper on walls of room
- Markers for participants
- Masking tape

Briefing

As participants come in, ask them to fill in the blanks on the chart paper.

Process

1. Place a category at the top of each chart paper:
   a. Name
   b. City of birth
   c. Astrological sign
   d. City of residence

   e. Favorite restaurant or type of food

   f. Hobby, leisure activity

   g. Expectation for the session

   h. Other, creative categories that will get people thinking and talking

2. Number the lines of Chart A with the number of participants.

3. Participants select a number on Chart A and then complete each chart using the same number, so their answers can be identified.

Debriefing

1. What do we have in common?

2. What are some of the differences we have?

3. What conclusions can you draw from the answers on the charts?

4. What questions do you have for group members?

Variations

Variation A

Have members stand and introduce themselves by adding to the information on the charts, such as where they work, why they are in the program.

Variation B

1. Divide the participants into random groups of four or five people.

2. Have each group list the following:

   a. What everyone in the group has in common

   b. Something unique about each member

   c. What they hope to achieve by the end of the program

   d. A name for the group

3. Each small group makes a brief presentation to the larger group.

Variation C

Add to the last page of the grid the category "Significant Family Value." Discuss the differences and similarities of family values, and how even when all the values appear to be positive and laudatory, in a common workplace, those values may conflict with one another or cause conflicts within the individual. For example, the values for honesty and courtesy often conflict because sometimes it is impossible to be honest and not hurt someone's feelings, which is considered discourteous.

ACTIVITY 2.4: SELF-IDENTITY PORTRAIT

This activity is a fun, creative way for participants to consider the many cultural groups to which they belong and to see how many cultures are represented in the group.

		Expertise of Facilitator		
		Low	Moderate	Extensive
Readiness of Group	Beginning			
	Intermediate		X	
	Advanced			

Purpose

To graphically describe one's cultural identity

Time Needed

45-60 minutes

Materials

- Markers
- One piece of chart paper for each person, or 8½ × 11 piece of paper

Briefing

Each of us belongs to a number of cultural groups. These groups reflect our ethnicity, our occupational and vocational cultures, and social groups that shape or reflect our values. Membership in a group is determined by how you identify with the group members as well as how those group members perceive you. On the paper you have been given, draw pictures, symbols, and diagrams that represent your cultural identity.

Process

1. Encourage each person to create a drawing that reflects the complexity of his or her cultural identity.
2. Have each person hang his or her drawing on the wall.

3. Let members mill around the room examining and discussing the drawings.
4. OR have each person explain his or her drawing to the entire group.

Debriefing

1. How did it feel to draw a picture of your culture?
2. How well did you represent yourself?
3. What have you learned about your colleagues?
4. What did you learn about culture?
5. How can you apply this knowledge?
6. Given the diversity represented by the drawings in the room, how can you explain your ability to get along with one another?
7. How can you use this information in the work you are doing?

Variation: My Cultural Identity

Ask participants to draw a diagram that reflects the various cultures with which they identify and that have influenced how they are perceived or how they perceive the world.

ACTIVITY 2.5: EXPLORING YOUR CULTURAL ROOTS

This activity helps introduce the historical context for Chapter 2 by providing participants the opportunity to retrace their family genealogy.

		Expertise of Facilitator		
		Low	*Moderate*	*Extensive*
Readiness of Group	Beginning			
	Intermediate		X	
	Advanced			

Purpose

To explore and share information about participants' individual cultures

Time Needed

60 minutes

Materials

None

Briefing

This activity will allow you to share elements of your cultural background and to learn from others about their cultural backgrounds using a specific set of cultural markers. Focus on your family of origin, the place where you grew up. Think about how you were in that family. As far back as you can remember, describe these aspects of your family: education, income, wealth, food.

Process

1. Give the group about 5 minutes to reflect quietly about families. Some participants may choose to take notes.
2. Allow each person 5 minutes to tell his or her story, beginning with the current generation and tracing as far back in the family as possible. You can control the amount of time

for this activity by organizing the participants into small groups.

3. Continue around the group until each person has had the opportunity to share his or her story.

4. Listen and compare and contrast, from one generation to the next and from individual to individual within the group.

Debriefing

1. If you have several small groups, they will not all complete at the same time. Circulate among the groups and engage them in initial debriefing by inviting them to share reactions, insights, and observations about the activity.

2. Once all groups have completed, spend a few minutes having the total group continue the debriefing begun in Step 1.

3. Ask for volunteers to share one insight to their own culture that was confirmed through their involvement in this activity.

4. Similarly, ask for members to share any new insights to their own culture that this activity provided.

5. Ask for volunteer members to share one thing that they learned about a fellow participant whom they have known for some time.

6. Ask for volunteer members to indicate the similarities and differences that they experienced among group members.

7. Finally, ask group members to consider how this activity influences their work with other educators, parents, and students.

Variation

Ask participants to answer the question, "When did you first become aware of yourself as a cultural entity?"

ACTIVITY 2.6: CULTURAL PERCEPTIONS

This activity is a significant way to introduce stereotyping in a low-key, nonthreatening manner. Understanding the process of stereotyping is an important step in fully using the information in Chapter 2.

		Expertise of Facilitator		
		Low	Moderate	Extensive
Readiness of Group	Beginning			X
	Intermediate			
	Advanced			

Purpose

To be used as an opening warm-up activity, as a way to test assumptions, and to introduce the concept of stereotyping

Time Needed

20 minutes

Materials

- Copies of the Cultural Perceptions handout (Figure A2.6.1)

Briefing

This activity will test your intuition and perceptions.

Process

1. Have participants select as a partner someone they don't know well or they would like to get to know better.
2. Using Figure A2.6.1, have the first partner share his or her perceptions of how the second partner would respond to each of the stems.
3. After the first partner shares his or her perceptions, the second partner gives his or her responses.
4. Switch roles and repeat the process.

Cultural Perceptions

Select for your partner someone that you don't know well, or who you would like to know better. Use the list below to share your perceptions. Ask your partner to give you his or her responses. Then switch roles and have your partner share his or her perceptions with you.

1. Country of family origin and heritage
2. Language(s) spoken
3. Interests or hobbies
4. Favorite foods
5. Type of movies, TV programs preferred, if any
6. Type of music preferred
7. Pet(s), if any, or favorite animals

Figure A2.6.1. Handout Sample

Debriefing

1. Reassemble the group and ask for volunteers to share their experiences in learning about another person.

2. Which assumptions were accurate? Which were not accurate?

3. Ask how it felt to have the responsibility for making the perceptions; how it felt being on the receiving end of the perceptions; and, what insight this gives to the process of stereotyping.

4. Ask how this informs us of the stereotyping that may occur when we face new teachers, aides, students, and parents.

5. How are stereotypes helpful? How are they harmful?

6. If the school is large, how are these perceptions enacted with people we rarely see?

7. What was the most important thing you learned from this experience?

8. How will you use this information?

ACTIVITY 2.7: CIRCLE OF STEREOTYPES

The concepts in this activity are important to understanding the emotional issues involved in Chapter 2. This activity is considered easier, or softer, than Personal Stereotypes (Activity 2.8) or Cultural Stereotypes (Activity 2.9).

		Expertise of Facilitator		
		Low	*Moderate*	*Extensive*
Readiness of Group	Beginning			
	Intermediate			X
	Advanced			

Purpose

To identify common stereotypes used with children and to experience how it feels to interact through the filter of someone's stereotype

Time Needed

40 minutes

Materials

- Construction paper suitable for making crowns
- Masking tape
- Markers
- Paper and pencils

Briefing

We are going to talk about how stereotypes affect our children. This activity is designed to have participants discuss how common stereotyping is in our everyday life and to realize the feelings often associated with the use of them.

Process

1. Divide the participants into two groups.
2. Give Group 1 the construction paper and tape. Ask it to make crowns for each member.

3. Ask Group 2 to generate a list of labels used to identify children, for example, *slow, very bright, nerd, teacher's pet, troublemaker, accident-prone, hostile.*

4. Have each person in Group 1 give his or her crown to someone in Group 2.

5. Have participants in Group 2 put one label on each crown, without showing the label to any members of Group 1.

6. Ask Group 1 to stand and form a circle facing out.

7. Ask Group 2 to form a circle around Group 1, with each member facing the person whose crown he or she is holding. Without showing the label, Group 2 crowns Group 1.

8. Members of Group 2 rotate one person to the right and talk to the person they are facing using language appropriate for the label on the crown the person is wearing. After a few moments, members of Group 1 rotate to the next person in the circle.

9. After each person in Group 1 has been addressed by each person in Group 2, have all the participants sit in a circle. Members of Group 1 continue to wear the crowns. They can see the labels of others but not of themselves.

Debriefing

1. Ask everyone in Group 1, individually, to talk about how they felt after listening to Group 2 speak to them and to guess what label was on their crown.

2. Ask members of Group 2 to comment on how they felt when addressing members of Group 1 and to describe how members of Group 1 reacted to the prejudicial comments.

3. How realistic are the labels? How frequently do you see them used?

4. What is the relationship of the labels to the ethnicity of students?

5. Is there anything wrong with the positive stereotypes used?

6. What did you learn from this activity?

7. How are you going to use what you learned?

Variation

For mature groups, try putting the names of various ethnic groups on the crowns. Describe specific situations, such as "at a school social function" or "in a disciplinary interview," and rotate the circles.

ACTIVITY 2.8: PERSONAL STEREOTYPES

In terms of impact, this activity is midway between the softer Circle of Stereotypes (Activity 2.7) and the harder Cultural Stereotypes (Activity 2.9). As with the other two activities, this illustrates the process of stereotyping that is important to understanding Chapter 2.

		Expertise of Facilitator		
		Low	*Moderate*	*Extensive*
Readiness of Group	Beginning			
	Intermediate			X
	Advanced			

Purpose

To identify the stereotypes associated with different kinds of people and to examine how stereotyping affects communication and self-esteem

Time Needed

30 minutes

Materials

- Several large Post-it notes for each person

Briefing

This activity will help you see how everyone is confronted with stereotypes.

Process

1. Ask each person to make of a list of the socio-cultural groups to which they belong and with which they associate painful stereotypes.

2. On one Post-it note, each person writes the name of one group, for example, "fat people," and places it on his or her chest.

3. Ask participants to *silently* walk around the room, reading the labels which have been written.

4. After everyone in the group has had a chance to read all the labels, ask them to organize themselves into small groups, based upon what they have written on their labels. For example, if only one person wrote "fat people," but several wrote labels that were related to body size—"too thin," "skinny legs," "big butt"—they can sit together in a group.

5. Ask the participants to discuss their labels and the stereotypes associated with each of them.

Debriefing

1. How did you feel writing and wearing the sterotypic comments?
2. What was it like to talk to others who suffer from the same or similar stereotypes?
3. How did you feel reading the stereotypes of others?
4. How do stereotypes impede healthy human relations?
5. How do they affect self-esteem?
6. How are stereotypes helpful?
7. What was the most important thing you learned from this exercise?
8. How will you use the information?

Variations

Rather than wearing the Post-it notes, sit in a semi-circle. Ask each person to come to the front of the room and to state the socio-cultural group and then the stereotypes associated with it. Move through the semi-circle quickly and without comment until everyone has spoken. Then discuss the process, the feelings, and what was learned.

ACTIVITY 2.9: CULTURAL STEREOTYPES

This activity will enrich discussion related to intergroup relationships introduced in Chapter 2. In contrast to Circle of Stereotypes (Activity 2.7) and Personal Stereotypes (Activity 2.8), this activity is the most challenging.

		Expertise of Facilitator		
		Low	*Moderate*	*Extensive*
Readiness of Group	Beginning			
	Intermediate			
	Advanced			X

Purpose

To identify the stereotypes associated with different groups and to examine how stereotyping affects communication and relationships

Time Needed

60 minutes

Materials

- Paper
- Pencils

Briefing

We are going to explore the stereotypes associated with the various ethnic groups to which we belong.

Process

1. Ask group members to sit with the people with whom they have the strongest ethnic identity. Trust the group to sort itself out. People may be uncomfortable at first, but if you give them time and no options, they will form appropriate groups.
2. In the groups, ask members to make a list of the common stereotypes held about their group.

3. Then ask group members to discuss the truth that has been overgeneralized to create that stereotype and what they want others not in their group to know about the stereotype.
4. Ask group members to identify additional information that they want others to know about their group.
5. Ask small groups to share with the larger group the essence of their discussions and the information they wish to teach or share.

Debriefing

1. How did you feel when you articulated the stereotypes about your group?
2. What was your response to the explanations of the stereotypes you heard?
3. Are there other stereotypes about which you have questions?
4. How do stereotypes impede healthy human relations?
5. How are stereotypes helpful?
6. What was the most important thing you learned from this exercise?
7. How will you use the information?

Variation

Separate participants by role, for example, classroom teachers, resource teachers, school administrators, district administrators; parents, teachers, students; or students, teachers, administrators; and conduct the activity.

ACTIVITY 2.10: ASSESSING
YOUR SCHOOL'S CULTURE

This activity will help reinforce the major concept of culture and its manifestations, as described in Chapter 2.

		Expertise of Facilitator		
		Low	*Moderate*	*Extensive*
Readiness of Group	Beginning			
	Intermediate			X
	Advanced			

Purpose

To identify the cultural expectations and the underlying values of a school

Time Needed

3 hours or more

Materials

- Chart paper
- Assessing the Culture of Your School handout (Figure A2.10.1)

Briefing

This activity will give us the opportunity to take a close look at the kind of school we are. We are going to articulate the unstated rules and values of this school in an attempt to see if who we say we are is who we really are.

Process

1. Review the definitions of culture, cultural expectations, overt values, and covert values as described in Chapter 2.
2. Organize participants into workgroups of 4 to 6 people. They may want to organize according to the grade levels or departments in which they work, or they may want to organize so that there is a representative of each grade level or department in each group. The former strategy will

reveal aspects of the subcultures in the school. The latter strategy will enable people to hear and explore different perceptions and experiences of the same school.

3. Provide each group with two sheets of chart paper, markers, and Figure A2.10.1.

4. Allow 30 minutes initially, checking to see how much additional time the groups need. It will take about 1 hour for the groups to explicate in detail the many aspects of the school's culture.

5. While the groups are working, make sure that they are writing the real values, that is, the rules of behavior that reflect the way things are, rather than the way they would like things to be.

Debriefing

When articulating the unspoken rules of a culture, participants are often disturbed by how negative their descriptions of the school, and consequently themselves, are. To debrief this activity effectively, it is important to acknowledge the discomfort some of the participants may have. It is equally important to provide adequate time for the debriefing of the information gathered. Before starting the process, review the following typical approaches people take when discussing their culture and indicate that you will remind participants gently when their presentations begin to reflect these nonproductive approaches.

1. *Make Nice.* Whatever is said, speakers will use words to obfuscate, mute, or nullify their statements.

2. *Deny.* In response to the speaker's truth, participants will deny that the rule exists or that such activities take place in this school.

3. *Make Excuses.* Participants will justify the existence of a rule to rationalize its existence.

4. *Defend.* Similarly, participants may want to defend the existence of a rule because it has filled a need personally, for the school, or for a group within the school.

Assessing the Culture of Your School

The culture of a school can be examined using a number of different models. This model easily adapts to most schools and groups. Use it to assess the culture and identify the cultural expectations of your school.

- **Heroes, sheroes, and their legends:** The stars of the school and the stories that are told about them that underscore the organizational value the stars exemplify

- **Rituals:** Routine activities that reinforce the values because they establish predictable patterns of behavior

- **Ceremonies:** Special rituals that celebrate the rites of passage of the members of the school, reinforce the values of the school, and acknowledge the heroes and sheroes

- **Play:** Activities that provide an outlet for anger and a release from day-to-day tensions and frustrations. What is considered funny? How do group members joke around? What is laughed at?

- **Communication and language:** The process of interacting and sharing information. Special vocabularies used by the members of the group.

- **Signs, symbols, and sacred spaces:** The tangible indicators of the school's norms and values. These also include the special places set aside for the heroes and sheroes within the school, for example teacher of the year awards, senior quad, and spelling bee plaques. Signs are sometimes used to mark or identify group members.

- **Values—overt and covert:** Overt rules are the things that we say we are. Covert rules are the "hidden curriculum"—the rules that we actually abide by. How does the school treat its students, its parents, and its teachers and aides in regard to
  - **Relationships:** What are the roles played by members of the group?
  - **Economics:** Psychic pay, perquisites (perks), resource distribution and allocation. What is the currency of exchange within the group? What is wealth and how is it acquired and used?
  - **Education:** Which is valued most—formal schooling, experience in the field, length of service within the school? How is information acquired? What kind of information is valued?
  - **Politics:** Who has the power? How is it acquired and shared?
  - **Ethics:** Morals. How are right and wrong, good and bad defined? What is the ethos of the school?
  - **Aesthetics:** What is considered to be beauty and how is it displayed in the physical environment?

Figure A2.10.1. Handout Sample

Adapted from Deal and Kennedy (1982).

ACTIVITY 2.11: ETHNIC PERCEPTIONS

This is an activity for mature participants and an experienced facilitator.

		Expertise of Facilitator		
		Low	*Moderate*	*Extensive*
Readiness of Group	Beginning			
	Intermediate			
	Advanced			X

Purpose

To help members of various ethnic groups identify and examine stereotypes held by group members and members of other ethnic groups

Time Needed

3 hours

Materials

- Chart paper
- Break-out rooms for each group

Briefing

We are going to examine stereotypes that you hold about your group and about other groups.

Process

1. Ask participants to self-select into ethnic groups. Members of the group they choose to join can question a participant's choice; however, others, including the facilitator, cannot.
2. Each group gets two sheets of paper to describe themselves:
   - How we see ourselves
   - How we think you see us

Each group gets an additional sheet of paper for each other's ethnic group:
- Group name
- How we see you

3. Allow 15 minutes for each question a small group has to answer. For example, if there are four small groups, each group will need 75 minutes for this step, (15 for your group and 15 minutes for each other group).

4. Provide each group with sufficient privacy to complete the activity in an open and honest manner.

5. Have each group return to the original meeting area and arrange chart paper panels by ethnic groups.

6. Participants are to mill around and read the work of all groups. This may take from 15 to 30 minutes depending on the size of the group.

7. Have each ethnic group meet again and discuss feelings, reactions, and observations about their own and others' data. Allow 10-20 minutes.

8. Have the total group reassemble and summarize reactions to the data about each group and other groups. Invite participants to ask questions to clarify. Allow 15 minutes per group.

9. Lead the group in discussing reactions, observations, and learning from the activity.

Debriefing

1. Example questions:
   a. What was it like to be in your ethnic-specific group?
   b. What issues were raised when you were asked to join an ethnic-specific group?
   c. What are your reactions to the way in which your own group viewed itself?
   d. What are your reactions to how similar or different your perceptions of your group compared with how other groups viewed your group?
   e. What do you see as differences or similarities among how groups are viewed?
   f. How will you be able to use this information in your school?

2. Invite participants to
   a. Write, in journal fashion, how this activity affected them

b. Engage in dialogue with colleagues about ways in which they may use this information
c. Discuss with colleagues the ramifications of these ethnic perceptions on interactions with parents, the community, students, and teachers

Variation

If the facilitator and participants agree that each group can honestly and authentically share their reactions to the information on the charts, Step 6 of the process may be eliminated.

ACTIVITY 2.12: THE CULTURAL PROFICIENCY CONTINUUM

This activity provides participants the opportunity to work with the first four points on the continuum and allows them to own the information by applying it to their own school situations.

		Expertise of Facilitator		
		Low	*Moderate*	*Extensive*
Readiness of Group	Beginning			
	Intermediate		X	
	Advanced			

Purpose

To identify examples of the points on the continuum

Time Needed

20 minutes

Materials

- Chart paper
- Marking pens
- Masking tape, or
- Transparencies, pens, and overhead projector

Briefing

Let's look at the cultural proficiency continuum, presented in Chapter 2, to see what meaning it has in our lives. We are going to develop some examples of the points on the cultural proficiency continuum.

Process

1. Divide participants into four groups.
2. Assign one of the first four points on the continuum to each group.

3. Ask participants to generate examples for each of the four points: cultural destructiveness, cultural incapacity, cultural blindness, cultural precompetence.
4. Have participants organize their lists of examples: district policies and practices; school policies and practices; classroom statements, actions.
5. If using chart paper, have participants post findings and mill around and look at one another's work. If using an overhead projector, have participants present their work in turn.

Debriefing

1. What questions of clarification do you have for the other groups?
2. What trends do you see across the data?
3. What do these examples say about the work that must be done in this district or school?
4. How does it feel to look at the district in this way?

Variation

Focus the discussion on classroom behavior.

✛ RESOURCE B: Activities for Chapter 3 ✛

ACTIVITY 3.1: MY WORK VALUES

Effective leadership can take place only when the values of the group are acknowledged.

		Expertise of Facilitator		
		Low	*Moderate*	*Extensive*
Readiness of Group	Beginning	X		
	Intermediate			
	Advanced			

Purpose

- To identify individual values that affect the workplace
- To increase awareness of how individually positive values may cause conflict in the workplace

Time Needed

60-90 minutes

Materials

- Chart paper
- Markers
- Masking tape

Briefing

Think about lessons you learned in your parents' home. What were the values on which those lessons were based? Identify three values that you learned at home and that you bring to the workplace. Share how these values affect your perceptions and relationships at work.

Process

1. Organize the participants into small groups of 3-5 people. Encourage the participants to diversify their groups.

2. Model for the group three values that you learned from your parents or the family in which you grew up and still use in the workplace. For example: get an education, be nice to your siblings, don't get pregnant. This translates today into my expectation that everyone will want to learn and be glad to go to training; that people will be especially courteous to the people they work with; and that they will be responsible for the consequences of their actions.

3. Clarify for the participants that in the small groups, they do not need to agree with all the values shared.

4. After participants have shared in the small groups, ask them to chart their values. Hang the charts around the room.

Debriefing

1. Each group shares the values and the stories that explain them for the members.

2. Discuss the apparent similarity of the values despite cultural, generational, or other differences.

3. Identify how values that in isolation are perceived as positive may clash and cause conflicts with the values of other people. For example: get an education and education is a privilege. Both of these are positive but will result in very different expectations and attitudes about learning.

ACTIVITY 3.2: STORYTELLING

This activity is useful in introducing members of leadership teams to one another in personal and meaningful ways.

		Expertise of Facilitator		
		Low	*Moderate*	*Extensive*
Readiness of Group	Beginning	X		
	Intermediate			
	Advanced			

Purpose

- To get acquainted with each other
- To gain some insight into participants' leadership styles

Time Needed

60 minutes

Materials

None

Briefing

Chapter 3 discusses leadership in the context of the many illustrations of personal and organizational culture. This activity introduces you to one another in terms of individual culture. This activity also will help you to learn more about your team members so that each of you will be more effective in both your nonformal and your formal leadership roles.

Process

1. Divide the group into work teams.
2. Ask the team members to form dyads with the person who they know least well.
3. Ask people to talk to their partners to find out something new about that person.

4. Have each team member tell a story about himself or herself that reveals something that the partners do not know.
5. Have each person share his or her partner's story with the team.
6. Have one member of the group synthesize the stories for the entire group.

Debriefing

1. What did you learn?
2. What conclusions can you draw about the members of your group?
3. What differences did you notice between the different teams?
4. What do the teams have in common?
5. How can you use this information in the work you will be doing?

Variation

Tell the story of when you
- Became aware of your culture
- First felt a need to serve the community
- Became an activist/passivist/and so on
- Decided to change your career
- Knew you were a leader
- Knew you didn't want to be a leader

ACTIVITY 3.3: THE GREAT EGG DROP

		Expertise of Facilitator		
		Low	Moderate	Extensive
Readiness of Group	Beginning		X	
	Intermediate			
	Advanced			

Purpose

- To build a sense of team spirit
- To create awareness of how resources are used
- To begin a conversation about collaboration and pooling resources

Time Needed

90 minutes-2 hours

Materials

- One copy of the directions sheet (Figure B3.3.1) for every participant
- A chair or raised area from which a person can drop the raw egg
- A hard surface, such as concrete or tile, on which to drop the eggs
- A large garbage bag to protect the floor when the eggs are dropped
- For each team: one raw egg, 23 plastic straws (preferably those without flexible tops), and 23 inches of masking tape
- Chart paper and a marker for keeping score

Briefing

This activity will help you learn how you work as a team and use your team's resources.

Process

1. Distribute Figure B3.3.1 and the team materials.

The Great Egg Drop Directions

Your task is to design a delivery system that will protect one raw egg dropped from a height of approximately 8 feet.

Your challenge is to achieve this goal using the least amount of resources. Your resources are limited to 23 straws and 23 inches of masking tape. *You may not use any other materials,* and catching the egg, boiling the egg, or removing its contents are not allowed.

In addition to constructing your product, the product must have a name, and you will be expected to deliver a brief creative presentation highlighting the benefits and features of your design.

All groups have been given the same task.

Scoring Criteria

Resources: 1 point for each straw or inch of tape left over

Marketing: Other teams will score your marketing pitch from 0 to 10: 10 is best. All the teams must agree on the score that they give your team.

Product: 0 points if the delivery system doesn't work; 44 if it does

Resources + Marketing + Product = Total

(23 + 23) + 10 + 44 = 100 possible points

Figure B3.3.1 Handout Sample

2. Allow each team to work for about 20 minutes.
3. Gather each team and have it present, one at a time, its environment and marketing pitch.
4. Obtain a consensus from the other teams regarding how many points to award for the name and marketing strategy.
5. Drop the egg and its environment from a height of about 8 feet.
6. Add points if the egg does not break.
7. Keep the scores on chart paper.

Debriefing

1. Give each team time to assess its process. Ask them to answer the following questions:
   a. How was the leader selected?
   b. What was your process for making decisions?
   c. Did everyone agree on the process?

    d. Did everyone participate?

    e. What roles did people play?

    f. What problems did you encounter? How did you resolve them?

    g. Did you win? How do you know?

2. Ask each team to summarize its group assessment and share it with the large group.

3. Ask the following questions, and others that occur to you, as they relate to the various tasks the teams were assigned.

    a. How does your behavior on this team compare to the work you have done on other teams?

    b. On what basis did you choose to use or reserve your resources?

    c. Did it occur to anyone to pool resources with another team?

    d. What have you learned that you can apply to your work on teams?

Variation

Tell the participants that the egg represents their school and the tape and straws are the resources they have to protect the quality of the education the school provides while building the cultural proficiency of the school.

ACTIVITY 3.4: CULTURAL PROFICIENCY CONSENSUS

This activity helps participants learn to apply the values of cultural proficiency in the school setting.

		Expertise of Facilitator		
		Low	*Moderate*	*Extensive*
Readiness of Group	Beginning			
	Intermediate			X
	Advanced			

Purpose

- To develop with participants a common language and understanding of cultural proficiency

- To provide participants an opportunity to discuss issues and concerns about cultural proficiency

Time Needed

45 minutes

Materials

- Cultural Proficiency Consensus Worksheet (Figure B3.4.1)
- Chart paper
- Markers

Briefing

This activity will help you clarify your understanding of cultural proficiency.

Process

1. Distribute copies of Figure B3.4.1 and ask each participant to complete it.
2. Divide the participants into groups of 4 and ask them to arrive at consensus decisions for each of the items. You may

---

Cultural Proficiency Consensus Worksheet

Please indicate whether you believe the following statements to be true or false.

_____ 1. Cultural proficiency recognizes that each individual is worthwhile and unique.

_____ 2. Culturally proficient education recognizes that each individual has dignity and integrity.

_____ 3. Skin color, language differences, sexual orientation, and other marks of difference are unimportant.

_____ 4. Students in U.S. schools need to learn to speak, write, and read standard forms of English.

_____ 5. School curricula should deal directly with the differences among people.

_____ 6. Educators should be taught to understand the cultural diversity of our society.

_____ 7. Parents and community people should help in planning and implementing a culturally proficient curriculum.

_____ 8. Schools should correct the differences found among students so that everybody in the United States learns to behave the same way.

_____ 9. Members of distinct cultural groups (e.g., ethnic, racial, gender, sexual orientation, job) have the same attitudes and values.

_____ 10. Education that values cultural proficiency serves only to divide people who are different.

Figure B3.4.1. Worksheet Sample

want to offer guidelines for consensus decision making, such as:

- Be forthright in expressing your perspectives and opinions.
- Risk listening to others' perspectives and opinions.
- Define consensus as a decision that each person can support.
- Avoid conflict-reducing techniques such as majority vote, averaging, or trading to reach decisions.
- Avoid changing your mind only to reach agreement and avoid conflict.

- View conflict as an opportunity to see others' viewpoints rather than as a hindrance to decision making.

3. Chart the consensus decision of each small group.
4. Lead a discussion of the responses by asking the spokesperson of each group to share his or her group's rationale for its answer. Once each group has given its response, give the preferred response and accompanying rationale (Figure B3.4.2).
5. Conduct an open discussion about the activity.

Debriefing

1. What was your initial reaction to the activity?
2. What were your experiences in the small group discussion?
3. Describe your levels of comfort in discussing your answers with people who had similar views, and with those who had dissimilar views.
4. How did your group deal with conflict?
5. What did you learn about the concepts and values associated with cultural proficiency?
6. How will you use this information?

Cultural Proficiency Consensus Preferred Responses

1. **True.** In this country, the goal of culturally proficient education is to recognize that each individual is unique and worthwhile. Although some so-called multicultural curricula may not achieve this goal, it is the goal of culturally proficient education and one toward which, we believe, all educators should be working.

2. **True.** This statement is an outgrowth of and consistent with Statement 1. Though the state-of-the-art in curriculum and instruction may not achieve this goal, it does not detract from the reaction of one's dignity and integrity.

3. **False.** Marks of difference may be unimportant to those who do not have them. Such people may think they judge others independent of these marks of difference. These marks of difference are important to those who have them, however. Not only do these marks of difference influence one's positive self-identity, they often serve as the basis for experiencing stereotyping or difference.

4. **True.** To have equity of opportunity in schools, business, or society in general, people must be able to speak, read, and write standard forms of English. This statement in no way detracts from the need for bilingual or multilingual skills. Every child who comes to school speaking a language other than standard English deserves to be respected for that language difference and to receive instructional support for maintaining that language. Likewise, native English-speaking children should learn an additional language.

5. **True.** This statement could serve as a corollary to Statements 1 and 2. Of course, the statement does not deny the appropriateness of dealing with people's similarities.

6. **True.** To achieve the goals of a culturally proficient education, administrators, teachers, and school support personnel need to learn about diversity in our society.

7. **True.** Parents and community members can be valuable resources in setting school goals that embrace culturally proficient values. They can also assist in developing guidelines for the implementation of goals and in evaluating those goals.

8. **False.** Patently untrue. This may have been a hoped-for goal for those touting the melting pot myth. A value of culturally proficient education is that there is strength in diversity and that the appreciation of difference is a realistic goal in this country. The reality of our country is that differences among U.S. citizens are obvious, and if we are to continue to serve all sectors, then we must positively reflect the benefits of those differences.

Figure B3.4.2 Handout Sample

9. **False.** An obvious stereotype. There exists the same degree of heterogeneity within groups that exists among groups. This becomes an important point of discussion when examining the compounding effects of class and caste (more fully developed in Chapter 5).

10. **False.** Quite the contrary; cultural proficiency is not adversarial. A major goal of culturally proficient education is to support people in seeing what we have in common in this country, how we can respect our differences, and what it takes to provide education to all people.

Figure B3.4.2. *Continued*

ACTIVITY 3.5: HUMAN RELATIONS NEEDS ASSESSMENT

		Expertise of Facilitator		
		Low	*Moderate*	*Extensive*
Readiness of Group	Beginning			X
	Intermediate			
	Advanced			

Administration and Analysis

The Human Relations Needs Assessment Instrument (Table B3.5.1) surveys a respondent's opinion about cultural relations in a school. Items are to be arranged in random sequence for administration. For analysis purposes, items are arranged into five factors: value for diversity; assessment of cultural knowledge; managing the dynamics of difference; institutionalizing cultural knowledge; and adapting to diversity.

The instrument can be used at least two ways. First, it can be administered to a group as pre-post measures to guide how a group is progressing in regard to the five factors. Second, it can be used to contrast the opinions among groups (e.g., educators, students, parents, businesspeople). However you choose to use the instrument, it should never be used as a diagnostic instrument, only as information to guide a school's planning.

We used the instrument with an entire school district where the data were used in combination with other data collection activities. For instance, in that district, we also audited district policies through document analyses and selected personnel interviews; we conducted a curriculum and instruction audit by reviewing documents, conducting interviews, and making school visits; and we analyzed newspaper and archival materials for the past 15 years. All data were analyzed using three sets of criteria: the district's core values, the five essential elements of cultural proficiency, and our posing the question, "How are they doing?" These data then became the frame for commendations and recommendations regarding district policies and procedures, curriculum and instruction, school relationships, and community relationships.

Currently, we are using the instrument at a university in combination with other data collection instruments and techniques to gauge the progress of students in a 24-unit intercultural proficiency program. This project is developing a model for educating both graduate and undergraduate students to become culturally proficient and for developing an interdisciplinary curriculum capacity for cultural proficiency.

TABLE B3.5.1 Human Relations Needs Assessment Instrument

1 = Rarely, 2 = Occasionally, 3 = Sometimes, 4 = Often, 5 = Usually

A Value for Diversity	*School Districts Should . . .*	*The District Does . . .*
1. Have a formal selection process for materials that have culturally diverse images	1 2 3 4 5	1 2 3 4 5 NA
2. Display materials that have culturally diverse images	1 2 3 4 5	1 2 3 4 5 NA
3. Sponsor activities to encourage making acquaintances with people of different cultural groups	1 2 3 4 5	1 2 3 4 5 NA
4. Take overt actions to hire people at all levels to represent a diverse workforce	1 2 3 4 5	1 2 3 4 5 NA
5. Establish policies that support diversity	1 2 3 4 5	1 2 3 4 5 NA
6. Promote activities that value the commonalities among people	1 2 3 4 5	1 2 3 4 5 NA
7. Promote activities that recognize that there are differences within ethnic groups	1 2 3 4 5	1 2 3 4 5 NA
8. Promote activities that recognize that each ethnic group has its own strengths and needs	1 2 3 4 5	1 2 3 4 5 NA

A Capacity for Cultural Assessment	*School Districts Should . . .*	*The District Does . . .*
1. Have a policy against racist and sexist jokes, slurs, and language	1 2 3 4 5	1 2 3 4 5 NA
2. Impose sanctions on those who use racist or sexist jokes, slurs, and language	1 2 3 4 5	1 2 3 4 5 NA
3. Provide opportunities for people to describe their cultural groups to others	1 2 3 4 5	1 2 3 4 5 NA
4. Teach people the effect that their ethnicity and gender has on those around them	1 2 3 4 5	1 2 3 4 5 NA

An Awareness of the Dynamics of Cultural Interaction	*School Districts Should . . .*	*The District Does . . .*
1. Teach people how to ask others appropriately about their cultural practices	1 2 3 4 5	1 2 3 4 5 NA
2. Acknowledge that conflict is a normal phenomenon	1 2 3 4 5	1 2 3 4 5 NA
3. Use known strategies for intervening in conflict situations	1 2 3 4 5	1 2 3 4 5 NA
4. Teach collaborative problem-solving techniques	1 2 3 4 5	1 2 3 4 5 NA
5. Regularly review policies to ensure that there are no subtle discriminatory practices	1 2 3 4 5	1 2 3 4 5 NA
6. Hold educators accountable for demonstrating high expectations	1 2 3 4 5	1 2 3 4 5 NA

TABLE B3.5.1 *Continued*

1 = Rarely, 2 = Occasionally, 3 = Sometimes, 4 = Often, 5 = Usually		
An Institutionalized Cultural Knowledge	*School Districts Should . . .*	*The District Does . . .*
1. Provide opportunities for learning about one's own culture	1 2 3 4 5	1 2 3 4 5 NA
2. Provide opportunities for learning about others' cultures	1 2 3 4 5	1 2 3 4 5 NA
3. Provide classes on different cultures for all students	1 2 3 4 5	1 2 3 4 5 NA
4. Provide workshops on different cultures for all employees	1 2 3 4 5	1 2 3 4 5 NA
5. Have policies that mandate learning about other ethnic groups	1 2 3 4 5	1 2 3 4 5 NA
6. Teach that ethnic groups often communicate in different ways	1 2 3 4 5	1 2 3 4 5 NA
7. Teach how to acknowledge the differences among people based on ethnicity	1 2 3 4 5	1 2 3 4 5 NA
8. Teach how to acknowledge the differences among people based on gender	1 2 3 4 5	1 2 3 4 5 NA
9. Provide a process for developing cultural understanding among all groups	1 2 3 4 5	1 2 3 4 5 NA
10. Ensure that the cultural groups within the community are represented on advisory groups (e.g., PTA)	1 2 3 4 5	1 2 3 4 5 NA
11. Ensure that the cultural groups within the community are represented in decision-making groups	1 2 3 4 5	1 2 3 4 5 NA

An Adaptation to Diversity	*School Districts Should . . .*	*The District Does . . .*
1. Have policies that prohibit discrimination	1 2 3 4 5	1 2 3 4 5 NA
2. Sanction, when appropriate, those whose behaviors conflict with practices that promote diversity	1 2 3 4 5	1 2 3 4 5 NA
3. Encourage students and school employees to talk about differences without making judgments	1 2 3 4 5	1 2 3 4 5 NA
4. Encourage cooperative learning strategies as a technique to get students to work and play together	1 2 3 4 5	1 2 3 4 5 NA
5. Teach students in their native language	1 2 3 4 5	1 2 3 4 5 NA
6. Employ and promote educators who reflect the ethnic and cultural makeup of the student body	1 2 3 4 5	1 2 3 4 5 NA

ACTIVITY 3.6: UNDERSTANDING
THE ESSENTIAL ELEMENTS

Purpose

To reinforce the essential elements of cultural competence and to begin the process of translating the concepts into individual behaviors and organizational practices

		Expertise of Facilitator		
		Low	Moderate	Extensive
Readiness of Group	Beginning		X	
	Intermediate			
	Advanced			

Briefing

Now that you have been introduced to the essential elements, let's see what cultural proficiency would look like at this school.

Materials

- Figure B3.6.1

Time Needed

40 minutes

Process

1. Introduce the essential elements of cultural proficiency.
2. Divide the participants into groups of 3 to 5 people.
3. Assign each group one element from Figure B3.6.1 to work on.
4. Ask each group to describe the behaviors of an individual or the practices of the school that reflect the particular element it is working on. Encourage groups to be as specific as possible.
5. When each small group is finished, ask it to share its responses with the entire group and have the other participants add to the list of behaviors and practices.

Activities to Reinforce the Essential Elements of Cultural Proficiency

1. **Value diversity.**
   - Recognize difference as diversity rather than inappropriate responses to the environment.
     Respect personal space.
     Accept culture of students and explain the school's culture.
     Celebrate the languages of LEP students.
     Stay open-minded to various experiences.
     Create an opportunity for managers and participants to express their fears, concerns, and anxieties and address them.
     Work with managers to develop job descriptions with clearly defined tasks and performance expectations.
     Send a profile sheet introducing new faculty or staff. Highlight some of his or her accomplishments. Identify what he or she hopes to contribute.
   - Accept that each culture finds some values and behaviors more important than others.
     Collectively define *value*.
     Share individual values.
     Share reasons for the importance of the values.
     Note and discuss similarities.
     Acknowledge differences in work performance attitudes.
     Develop the necessary training programs to develop skills and abilities.
     Develop a screening process to identify individuals with appropriate skills and backgrounds to match the organization's needs.

2. **Assess cultural values.**
   - Have a real sense of your individual culture.
     Use films, videos, and other resources to show different cultures.
     Role-play and use drama, songs, and books.
     Have students share their feelings about their classroom.
     Have focus groups to discuss cultural issues.
     Exercise: "What I hold near and dear."
     Exercise: "My Cultural Identity Circle."
     Exercise: "My Family Cultural Values."
     Identify staff who speak other languages.
     Have parents, teachers, and students share their values and cultures.
   - Understand how your culture or the culture of your school affects those whose culture is different.
     Give students a caretaker "buddy" of the same subculture or gender.
     Provide an orientation tour by the buddy, of restrooms, the bus, the lunchroom, the playground.

Figure B3.6.1 Sample Responses

Give responsibilities that include them as part of the group.

Inform staff of corporate culture to integrate with their own.

Establish a task force to assess culture.

Give the new member a seat, a place to be. Make him or her feel included by giving the person a name tag, a cubbyhole for storage, or whatever are normal individual properties.

Have students decide what is important to tell new students; institutionalize the orientation information.

Conduct a systems review—identify the practices and assumptions derived from practices and the beliefs or values based on those practices and assumptions.

Present case studies, resolve the situation, and examine values of the group that led them to the decision.

3. **Manage the dynamics of difference.**

   ■ Understand the effect that historic distrust has on present-day interactions.

   Issues of power and dominance affect all cultures through history to the present. Use time lines, role-play, role reversal, murals illustrating reactions to the distrust (e.g., migrations, insurrection), Venn diagrams and tables, narratives, poetry, essays (analysis), plays.

   Establish liaisons with cultural groups (e.g., schools, community center).

   ■ Realize that you may misjudge others' actions based on learned expectations.

   Acknowledge that it is okay not to be perfect.

   Ascertain people's motives for their actions before reacting.

   Use literatures from diverse cultures.

   Analyze significant historical events and discuss why people today may be resentful of these past situations.

   Drawing from students' cultural backgrounds, have them role-play situations that could be misunderstood.

4. **Institutionalize cultural knowledge.**

   ■ Incorporate cultural knowledge into the mainstream of the organization.

   Conduct inservice training.

   Compile school lists of community role models and speakers who can be invited to the classroom.

   Use parents.

   Provide seminars or workshops so that administrators and the board understand the importance of diversity.

   Include cultural diversity in the mission and values of the district. Teach about differences within cultures.

   Reflect the mission and vision in personnel policies and practices.

Figure B3.6.1 *Continued*

Increase the number of minority mentors.

Provide diversity training for all staff and volunteers.

- Develop skills for cross-cultural communication.

    Make it okay to ask questions to clarify cultural conundrums.

    Learn the language of clients and community.

    Learn cultural mores of other groups represented in the organization.

    Provide a written procedure manual that includes goals and objectives, specifically regarding diversity.

    Include diverse images in art and the environment.

5. **Adapt to diversity.**

    - Teach origins of stereotypes and prejudices.

        List

        Discuss

        Expose outcomes, ramifications

        Problem solve

    - Institutionalize cultural interventions for conflicts and confusion caused by the dynamics of difference.

        Teach cultural truths and facts that will cause understanding rather than encourage the perpetuation of negative stereotypes.

        Teach cultural holidays and why they are important.

        Establish cross-cultural mentoring.

        Provide formal training to share the organizational culture.

    - Accept that there will be times that everyone will be uncomfortable and realize it is a first step to growth.

    - Review policies, guidelines, and procedures for items of cultural incompetence.

    - Develop a system of conflict management in recognition that change creates stress or conflict and accept it as okay.

    - Seek out diversity through brainstorming techniques and going outside boundaries of comfort.

    - Begin the behavior knowing the attitude will follow.

Figure B3.6.1. *Continued*

Debriefing

1. How difficult was it to describe what each element would look like in our school?

2. Was it easier to describe individual behavior or organizational practices?

3. Did you notice whether people set standards for others or for themselves?

4. How would you like to use these lists?

Variations

1. Focus on a work group, a department, or a classroom.
2. Save the lists for use during schoolwide planning.
3. After further understanding the elements of cultural competence, add to the lists.

⚜ RESOURCE C: Activities for Chapter 4 ⚜

ACTIVITY 4.1: OBSERVATION ACTIVITY

Creating change in any school requires the development of a climate for change. The collection of data is one of the skills that is central to creating a climate for change. In this activity, you practice one of the first steps for collecting data, which is to hone the skills of observation as a technique for data collection.

		Skill of Facilitator		
		Low	*Moderate*	*Extensive*
Readiness of Group	Beginning		X	
	Intermediate			
	Advanced			

Purpose

To practice the skill of collecting data by observing

Time Needed

2 hours

Materials

- Observation questions (see Debriefing)
- Pencils

Briefing

Most of us ask questions when we want to know something. This activity will give you an opportunity to gather information and identify how much you can learn by simply observing.

Process

Instruct participants to go outside alone and to walk no more than 15 minutes away from the training site. They are to find a place to sit where they will not be obtrusive to the environment and where they will not be engaged in conversation. Then they are to sit for 30 minutes and observe what there is to see from that one spot.

Debriefing

When participants return, give them a sheet with the following questions to answer. Do not give the questions before participants go, because they will filter what they see. After they have answered the questions for themselves, have them discuss their answers either in small groups or in a large group.

1. How did you choose the site to observe?
2. What were your initial impressions?
3. What happened after you were sitting for about 10 minutes?
4. What did you see?
5. How did you interpret what you saw?
6. Did your interpretations change after you observed for several minutes?
7. Did you see anything that surprised you? Did your impressions change about anything?
8. What have you learned from this process
   a. About yourself?
   b. About what you observed?
   c. About the skill of observation?

Variations

1. Have participants go to a meeting or to a site for observation in the community in which they will conduct their project.
2. Have participants focus on looking for particular issues based on the concepts this activity is used to reinforce.

ACTIVITY 4.2: SIMULTANEOUS STORYTELLING

One of the key skills to creating change in schools is to develop ability in cross-cultural communications. This activity introduces the challenges that people often experience in not being heard.

		Skill of Facilitator		
		Low	*Moderate*	*Extensive*
Readiness of Group	Beginning			
	Intermediate		X	
	Advanced			

Purpose

To help participants understand how it feels to not be listened to

Time Needed

20 minutes

Materials

None

Briefing

Think of a time when you did something that was hard for you and you were very proud of your accomplishment. This may be something that no one else knows about or that is easy for most people to do. Think of a time when you overcame a personal barrier. Prepare to tell this story to a member of your group.

Process

Ask group members to sit with their teams. After they are situated, thinking they will each have a turn to tell their stories, instruct them to tell their stories now, ALL AT ONCE.

Debriefing

When the last person has told his or her story, ask the following questions:

1. How did you feel when you got the assignment? How did you select the story to tell?

2. How important was the story to you?

3. Have you ever told the story before?

4. How did you feel as you anticipated telling the story?

5. Did you expect the listener to empathize with you and understand how important this experience was to you?

6. What did you think when you got the instructions to tell your stories simultaneously?

7. How did it feel to tell the story with everyone else talking?

8. Have you had an experience similar to this one when you were talking but no one was listening?

9. Have you ever not listened when someone was trying to tell you something that was more important to them than it was to you? Often in cross-cultural communication, a person is so intent on telling his or her story that he or she does not hear, and therefore can neither understand nor empathize with the stories of others.

10. What have you learned from this activity?

11. How will you use what you have learned?

ACTIVITY 4.3: CROSS-CULTURAL COMMUNICATION

This activity provides participants with the opportunity to define how their cultural groups prefer to receive communication and to learn the same about other groups' communications preferences and styles

		Skill of Facilitator		
		Low	*Moderate*	*Extensive*
Readiness of Group	Beginning			
	Intermediate		X	
	Advanced			

Purpose

To articulate differences in communicating cross-culturally

Time Needed

2 hours

Materials

- Chart paper
- Markers

Briefing

This activity will give you an opportunity to share with the other participants information they need for talking effectively with members of your cultural group. It will give you a chance to shatter some stereotypes on one hand, but on the other hand it will allow you to share some useful generalizations.

Process

1. Have the group members sit with other members of their ethnic groups. If they want to divide into subgroups, allow them to do that. For example, if the African Americans want to divide into a middle-class, college-educated group and a working class, grassroots group, this may be useful.

2. Ask each group to list some rules, suggestions, and tips for interacting with that particular group. They may want to use some of these categories: initial approach; presenting oneself to the group (credentials, background, etc.); attitude toward time; introducing change; giving feedback; disagreeing; pointing out errors; things that help communication; things that impede communication.

   Encourage each group to discuss among itself the paradigms members might use for judging newcomers. What are the rules of discourse that they use when interacting with outsiders? What should a newcomer do if he or she wants to be accepted and listened to?

3. Allow each group to present its list.

Debriefing

Make sure you ask questions that clarify and underscore the subtle but important differences in the expectations of each group when communicating. Seek to determine whether one group has different expectations for different ethnic groups. Talk about clothing and appearance if you perceive this to be an important issue as well.

Variations

1. This exercise could be used to explore differences in cross-gender or intergenerational communication.

2. With a mature group and an experienced trainer, a similar activity could start by identifying "Things that are annoying or frustrating about talking with . . ."

ACTIVITY 4.4: PARADIGMS

		Skill of Facilitator		
		Low	*Moderate*	*Extensive*
Readiness of Group	Beginning			
	Intermediate		X	
	Advanced			

Purpose

To develop common language and a new perspective for viewing the change process

Time Needed

2 hours

Materials

- Chart paper
- Markers
- Video cassette player and monitor
- Video: *Paradigm Principles* (Barker, 1996)

Briefing

A paradigm is a set of rules or criteria that we use to judge the appropriateness or correctness of something. This video will help you explore the paradigms you use in your life. When it is over, we will discuss what paradigms affect the work we are doing in our school.

Trainer Note: Read the book review presented in Figure C4.4.1.

Process

Show video. Conduct discussion.

Debriefing

Assign debriefing questions to small groups. Each group can answer one question, or if you have more time, each group can answer all seven questions. As the groups present their responses, allow time for discussion, questions, and additions to each group's list by the other members in the class.

1. What paradigms do you want to keep at our school [in our district]?
2. What paradigms do you want to reject?
3. What paradigms are changing or shifting?
4. What paradigms have been challenged unsuccessfully?
5. What new paradigms do you predict will develop in the next few years?
6. What today is impossible, but if it could be done would fundamentally change the way we address issues of diversity?
7. What are the implications of the answers to these questions for your school?

Discovering the Future: The Business of Paradigms
by Joel Arthur Barker (1989)

Do you remember when polyester was a miracle fabric and "made in Japan" meant cheap and tacky? If you made lists called "working mother" or "father's jobs" in 1965, how would they differ from the same list written in 1993? These are examples of paradigms that have changed. A *paradigm* is the set of rules or criteria you use to judge whether something is correct or appropriate. A paradigm is a filter of perception; it is a frame you put around a concept to understand it and make it fit with your understanding of the world.

We all use paradigms to order our worlds. When we do a double-take because we have observed or experienced something odd, when we argue intensely against a new idea, it is because our paradigms have been challenged. Joel Barker is a futurist who has taken the concept of paradigm, used initially and solely by scientists, and reframed it for the world at large. He uses the concept of paradigms to help explain the process of change.

Most people resist change because they feel threatened. They fear that they may lose something that they value. The new idea or process does not fit within the boundaries of their current paradigms, so they resist or actively seek to prove the new idea is wrong, inappropriate, or unnecessary. *Paradigm shifters* are perceived as misfits or outcasts who move along the margins of the group. They may be older and venerated and therefore have no fear of losing their power or prestige, or they may be new and unseasoned, seeking to prove themselves to veterans in the field. *Paradigm resisters* are people who are vested in a system or who are among the system's elite. They have the greatest to lose and will be among those who denounce a proposed change most vociferously. They suffer from "hardening of the categories."

Joel Barker presents many interesting examples and lots of challenging questions as he explains how paradigms can be used to introduce and plan for change in an organization. Think about the values, habits, processes, and policies that direct your activities. These are your paradigms. As you prepare for changes in your life or your organization, ask yourself these questions:

1. What paradigms do you want to keep?
2. What paradigms do you want to reject?
3. What paradigms are changing or shifting?
5. What new paradigms do you predict for the organization?
6. What today is impossible, but if it could be done would fundamentally change the way you live?
7. What are the implications for the answers to your questions?

Figure C4.4.1. Book Reviews by Authors

ACTIVITY 4.5: ESSENTIAL ELEMENTS
OF CULTURAL PROFICIENCY

		Skill of Facilitator		
		Low	*Moderate*	*Extensive*
Readiness of Group	Beginning			
	Intermediate		X	
	Advanced			

Purpose

To practice applying the elements of cultural proficiency to the specific classroom culture

Time Needed

30 minutes

Materials

- A copy of the five essential elements of cultural proficiency (Figure 2.3)
- Chart paper and markers

Briefing

Now that we know what the five essential elements are, let's discuss how we can use them in our classroom.

Process

1. Distribute or post a copy of the essential elements of cultural proficiency (Figure 2.3).
2. Divide the participants into at least five small groups.
3. Assign one element to each group.
4. Ask the participants to brainstorm activities that can be implemented in the classroom.
5. When the lists are completed, have each group share its work and invite the other participants to respond to the lists with additions and critical comments.

6. Reinforce the different elements by asking participants to indicate whether they agree that an activity is related to the specific element being discussed.

Debriefing

Ask participants to discuss their level of comfort with the process of brainstorming activities. Then ask them to discuss what it would take to implement the activities. Finally, decide as a group what you will do with the lists of activities.

Variations

1. Reproduce and distribute the lists. Ask the group to refine them.
2. Assign committees to implement particular activities.
3. Repeat the activity focusing on the school or district culture.
4. Repeat the activity with different audiences (e.g., students, parents, teachers, staff). Compile the lists and refine them into a school plan.

ACTIVITY 4.6: 7-MINUTE DAY

This activity provides participants with the opportunity to integrate their skills in working with parents and other community members when confronting problem situations.

		Skill of Facilitator		
		Low	*Moderate*	*Extensive*
Readiness of Group	Beginning			
	Intermediate			X
	Advanced			

Purpose

To use role-playing to practice the skills of conflict resolution that arise from cultural misunderstandings

Time Needed

2 hours

Materials

- Chart paper
- Marking pens
- Copies of role descriptions (Figure C4.6.1) for each of the three role groups
- Copies of general instructions (Figure C4.6.2) for all participants
- Copies of 7-Minute Day Data Sheet (Figure C4.6.3) for all participants
- One room to serve as a communications center and three break-out rooms

Briefing

You will be engaged in a simulated role-playing situation in which you will have the opportunity to play roles other than your current school-related roles. This activity will give you the op-

---

7-Minute Day Roles

Administrators and board members: From your group, select participants to serve as board members, the superintendent, the business manager, the public information officer, the principal of the high school where the fight took place, a middle school principal, and an elementary school principal.

Teachers: Select officers for your local association. Designate your group members to be 70% white, 15% African American, 10% Latino, and 5% Asian Pacific Islander.

Parents: Designate your group members to be 40% Latino, 33% white, 20% African American, 5% Asian Pacific Islanders, and 2% other.

Figure C4.6.1 Handout Sample

portunity to experience how it feels to be a member of another group. You will also practice cross-cultural communications and problem-solving skills.

Process

1. To the extent possible, have teachers role-play administrators, board members, or parents of this school. Likewise, have parents play roles other than parents and board members; have administrators do the same.
2. Distribute and read aloud the general instructions (Figure C4.6.2). Respond to questions of clarification.
3. Distribute and read aloud the 7-Minute Day Data Sheet (Figure C4.6.3).

General Instructions
1. Use the initial 20-minute strategy session to develop your course of action. Record it on chart paper.
2. Select a message carrier. All communications are to be delivered to the communications center.
3. Develop responses to the other groups' messages and record them on newsprint during each 7-minute day.
4. Any group may move time ahead and skip a day by informing the other groups in writing.
5. Plan your strategies well.

Figure C4.6.2. Handout Sample

7-Minute Day Data Sheet

1. Your district has had a diversity plan in effect for 3 years. The plan had broad community support when it was first implemented.

2. Parents have recently expressed a concern that there is increasing violence and vandalism in the schools.

3. Teachers have filed grievances over the administration's lack of effective action in handling three recent assaults on teachers.

4. African American and Latino parents have charged the board of education and administration with unfair treatment of their children predicated on the high rate of suspensions and expulsions and their underrepresentation in honors classes.

5. Current student population is 40% Latino, 33% white, 20% African American, 5% Asian.

6. Current faculty population is 70% white, 15% African American, 10% Latino, 5% Asian.

7. A fight that occurred 2 days ago resulted in the suspension of three African American students, two white students, and two Latino students. They may be recommended for expulsion.

8. A small group of parents went to the school to protest the suspensions, and a heated interchange led to some pushing and shoving. This action led to the arrest of one white and one African American parent.

9. A group of angry parents are demanding that
    a. The board of education and the administration eliminate the racist practices in the school
    b. The suspended students be readmitted and their records be cleared
    c. All charges be dropped against the parents who were arrested

10. If the demands are not met, the parents will withdraw their students from the school, causing the district to lose finances because of the reduced average daily attendance allotment.

Figure C4.6.3. Handout Sample

4. Divide the group into the three role groups and situate them in separate rooms—parents, teachers, and administrators/board members. Distribute their role descriptions (Figure Rc.2) and respond to questions of clarification.

5. Provide the groups 20 minutes to do their initial planning.

6. At the end of the 20 minutes, announce, "This is the beginning of day 1" (you may want to designate it as a day of the week, such as Monday, October 14).

7. Have one room serve as communications center and receive and distribute messages as appropriate. You may just have to step aside and let the process unfold.

8. Announce every 7 minutes, "It is now day 2" or "It is now Tuesday, October 15." Repeat this process until you have enough information to have a productive discussion. Usually it takes only 4-6 days to provide enough information for a very informed discussion.

Debriefing

You can begin the debriefing process in either of two ways:

1. You can ask each group in turn to respond to the questions that follow.

2. You can have each group return to its break-out room and spend a few minutes charting answers to the questions and then return in 15-20 minutes and post responses.

Then ask the following questions:

1. What were your initial reactions/impressions when I described this activity?

2. How did you feel, as a member of your role group, during the planning phase of the activity?

3. How did you react to being a member of your role group during the conduct of the 7-minute days?

4. How do you react to the other two role groups? During the planning phase? During the 7-minute day phase?

5. What insights does this provide for the way we do business in schools?

6. What did you learn about your role group? What did you learn about the other role groups?

7. In what ways will you be able to use the information learned in this session?

8. In looking at the outcomes of your meeting, where do you judge them to be on the cultural proficiency continuum? What evidence do you have for your judgment?

9. How could you improve the process of your meeting, as well as the outcome of the meeting?

Variations

1. Add role groups, for example, students, business leaders, activist groups, other interest groups.

2. Select other issues that have more immediate relevance to your school.

ACTIVITY 4.7: PICK A SOCIAL EQUITY CELL

		Skill of Facilitator		
		Low	*Moderate*	*Extensive*
Readiness of Group	Beginning			
	Intermediate			X
	Advanced			

Purpose

To examine the issues and events presented in Table 4.1

Time Needed

45 minutes

Materials

- Copies of Table 4.1

Briefing

Let's take some time to talk about how the events presented in Table 4.1 have affected your own lives. This is a chance to make this chart come alive.

Process

1. Ask participants if there are any general questions about the chart. If they ask a question that you cannot answer, for example, "What do you mean by culturally marginal?" check to see if there are members of the group who may be able to respond.
2. Organize the participants into small groups of 4 to 6 people.
3. Ask people to select a cell in the chart that is particularly meaningful to them.
4. In turn, each person tells a story in response to the cell while the others listen, ask questions for clarification, or respond with stories of their own.
5. Allow 20-30 minutes for the small group interaction.

Debriefing

1. Summarize what happened in your small group.
2. What did you learn about yourself?
3. Do you understand your colleagues in a new way now?
4. Do you understand this chart differently or better now?
5. How will you use this information?

Variations

1. Assign to each small group a particular row to discuss.
2. Assign to each small group a particular column to discuss.
3. Assign to each group a particular cell to discuss.

ACTIVITY 4.8: GROUP STEREOTYPES

This activity invites people to acknowledge their unspoken prejudices and to recognize how often negative stereotypes are applied to every cultural group.

		Skill of Facilitator		
		Low	*Moderate*	*Extensive*
Readiness of Group	Beginning			
	Intermediate			X
	Advanced			

Purpose

To identify the stereotypes associated with different groups of people, and to examine how stereotyping impacts one's perceptions of others

Time Needed

60 minutes

Materials

- Several pieces of chart paper
- Large Post-it notes, about 20 for each participant

Briefing

This activity will help you to see how we stereotype other people.

Process

1. Label each piece of chart paper with one of these group categories: White women, White men, Black women, Black men, Hispanic women, Hispanic men, Gay men, Lesbians, etc.
2. Hang the charts around the room.
3. Give each participant a small stack of large Post-it notes.

4. Ask them to write labels and stereotypes they have heard used about each group.
5. Silently have the participants affix the Post-it notes to the appropriate chart.
6. Mill around and read what has been written.

Debriefing

1. How did you feel writing the stereotypes?
2. What did you think as you read what was written?
3. How did you feel as you read what was written?
4. What is your reaction to all these labels around the room?
5. What are the implications of this activity?
6. How will you use the information?

⁜ RESOURCE D: Activities for Chapter 5 ⁜

ACTIVITY 5.1: DEMOGRAPHICS

This activity provides participants with the opportunity to understand the magnitude of the diversity within the school community.

		Skill of Facilitator		
		Low	*Moderate*	*Extensive*
Readiness of Group	Beginning			
	Intermediate		X	
	Advanced			

Purpose

To identify the demographic makeup in a community

Time Needed

2 weeks. This activity will take place outside of a formal training room.

Materials

- A list of library reference materials
- A description of the process for gaining access to
  Newspaper files and resources
  Census bureau data
  District demographic data

Briefing

This process will familiarize you with the demographic makeup of your school's community.

Process

1. Divide the group into teams of 3 or 4 people.
2. As a large group, identify the major and minor ethnic groups represented in the district.

3. Brainstorm on how to gather information about a particular group of people: churches, cultural centers, libraries, newspaper libraries, specific social and civic organizations.

4. Let each team select a group about which it will gather demographic information.

5. Provide a list of minimally acceptable data: total population in city, total population in district, area of the city that is most densely populated with this group, socioeconomic status, languages spoken, resources for teachers about this group of people.

6. Challenge each team to find the most useful and interesting information about its group.

7. Discuss ethnically appropriate protocol and etiquette, so team members are not viewed as culturally incompetent intruders by other ethnic groups.

8. Describe the format in which the information should be presented.

Debriefing

Ask each team to present its information to the group in a way that is interesting and entertaining. As part of or after the presentation, ask each team to respond to these questions as well as others from members of the large group:

1. What did you learn about yourself in the process?
2. Did you have any serendipitous adventures?
3. What was the greatest challenge of this activity?
4. What was the greatest surprise?
5. How will you use what you have learned?

ACTIVITY 5.2: DIVERSITY LIFELINE

This activity provides a good introduction to Chapter 5 in that it helps to provide a context for entitlement.

		Skill of Facilitator		
		Low	*Moderate*	*Extensive*
Readiness of Group	Beginning			
	Intermediate		X	
	Advanced			

Purpose

- To have participants analyze and share the significant events in their lives that have affected their perception of diversity
- To aid participants in understanding that diversity is a dynamic that has been and will be ever present in their lives

Time Needed

90 minutes

Materials

- Chart paper
- Markers
- Masking tape
- Tables or floor space for participants to draw their lifelines
- Enough wall space for all participants to hang their lifelines and discuss them in small groups

Briefing

Think about your life and how you have been affected by your diversity and when you became aware of the diversity around you. On the chart paper, draw a graph of your life marking the significant points that reflect your awareness of diversity.

Process

1. Distribute markers and chart paper to each person.
2. Organize the participants into groups of 3 to 5 people. Encourage the participants to diversify their small groups.

It is important to keep the groups small so that each person can share extensively. It is also important that people in the small groups are comfortable with each other.

3. Allow about 20 minutes for participants to draw and hang their lifelines.

4. Allow about 15 minutes per person to describe his or her lifeline. This time will also include the response to questions from and reactions by group members.

5. Reorganize the small groups into one large group.

Debriefing

1. What did you learn about yourself from this process?
2. What did you learn about your group members?
3. What did you learn about diversity?
4. How will you use what you have learned?

Variations

1. Use the lifeline process to have participants tell their stories without emphasizing any particular aspect of their lives.
2. Cover the wall with chart paper. As a group, draw a lifeline for the organization.
3. Allow participants to draw their personal lines to indicate where their lives intersect with the life of the school.

ACTIVITY 5.3: DISCUSSION QUESTIONS
ABOUT U.S. HISTORY

This activity provides participants with the opportunity to understand seldom-discussed events in U.S. history and the effect they have on current cultural relations. The activity can be used to introduce or to summarize Chapter 5.

		Skill of Facilitator		
		Low	*Moderate*	*Extensive*
Readiness of Group	Beginning			
	Intermediate			X
	Advanced			

Purpose

To teach that issues of oppression have historical foundations in the history of our country

Time Needed

60 minutes

Materials

- A facilitator with a good grasp of U.S. history
- Copies of the discussion questions about U.S. history (Figure D5.3.1) for each participant
- At least one copy of the answer sheet (Figure D5.3.2) for the facilitator

Briefing

This activity will familiarize us with historical events in which U.S. citizens were treated with discrimination and the effect of these on our human relations today. To appreciate the concept of entitlement, a questionnaire will highlight some of the major concepts of Chapter 5.

(text continued on page 214)

Discussion Questions About U.S. History

The questions below are to be used as a discussion catalyst. Please read
and mark whether you believe them to be true or false. Some of the
questions are factual and call on your knowledge of U.S. history; others
may be matters of perspective and call on your ability to make judgments.
In a few minutes, you will be asked to discuss your answers with other
participants and to arrive at consensus responses.

_____ 1. Native American Indians have been remanded to reservations
in the United States.

_____ 2. Columbus discovered the Americas.

_____ 3. African Americans were guaranteed full citizenship status
with the enactment of the 14th Amendment to the U.S.
Constitution in 1868.

_____ 4. Jacksonian Democracy of the 1830s expanded voting rights to
nonlandowners.

_____ 5. Women were granted the right to vote with the enactment of
the 19th Amendment to the U.S. Constitution in 1920.

_____ 6. In the pre-Civil War United States, the only people who could
vote in national elections were white men.

_____ 7. U.S. citizens of Japanese ancestry were confined to relocation
camps during World War II.

_____ 8. History, as written in our textbooks, is factual and without bias.

_____ 9. Addressing issues of diversity is a process in which white men
can have a responsible role.

_____ 10. In our country's history, the practice of hiring and promoting
people usually has been predicated on selecting the most
qualified person.

_____ 11. Racism and sexism are institutional practices that have served
as barriers to people of color and women in our country.

_____ 12. Racism and sexism as institutional practices no longer exist in
this country.

_____ 13. One of the consequences of institutionalized racism and
sexism has been that people of color and women have been
kept out of the workforce and white men have benefited.

_____ 14. The melting pot concept was an effective process by which
many European immigrants, within two or three generations,
were blended into the U.S. mainstream society.

_____ 15. Many states in our country enacted Jim Crow laws that denied
people basic human rights based on their ethnicity.

_____ 16. Backlash is the angry and defensive reaction to programs and
laws that promote a diverse society.

Figure D5.3.1. Worksheet Sample

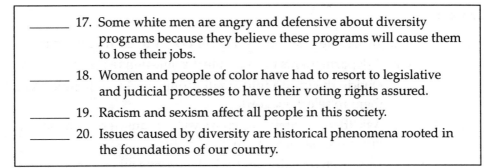

_____ 17. Some white men are angry and defensive about diversity programs because they believe these programs will cause them to lose their jobs.

_____ 18. Women and people of color have had to resort to legislative and judicial processes to have their voting rights assured.

_____ 19. Racism and sexism affect all people in this society.

_____ 20. Issues caused by diversity are historical phenomena rooted in the foundations of our country.

Figure D5.3.1. *Continued*

Answer Sheet and Commentary

Questions that have factual responses:

1. **True.** U.S. history is replete with such examples. Many make the argument that today many people stay on reservations due to the inducements to do so.
2. **False.** There were millions of people in the Americas when he arrived.
3. **True.** That was the intent of the legislation, though it was usurped throughout the United States.
4. **True.** Though it applied only to white males.
5. **True.** That was the intent of the legislation, though it, too, was usurped throughout the United States.
6. **True.**
7. **True.** Well over 100,000 U.S. citizens were denied basic rights of citizenship.
14. **True.** This was the genesis for the melting pot theory.
15. **True.** After the U.S. Civil War, states throughout the country devised ways to prevent African Americans from voting.
18. **True.** As indicated in the reponses to questions 4 and 5, women and people of color have had to use legal means to gain the right to vote in this country.

The balance of the questions will promote interesting discussion among the participants.

Question 8 may appear to be false at first reading but is, too often, the way educators and members of the community approach textual material.

Question 9 poses the moral dilemma referred to in the latter part of Chapter 5 and is a quite important topic.

Questions 10, 11, 12, 13, 16, 17, 19, and 20 ask a person to deduce from historical events the effects that these events or social forces had on the citizenry of this country.

Figure D5.3.2. Handout Sample

Process

1. Distribute one copy of Figure D5.3.1 to each participant.
2. Ask participants to complete the questions as best they can.
3. Divide the group into small groups of 4 to 6 people. Ask them to select a recorder.
4. Ask them to arrive at consensus on answers to as many questions as they can in 20 minutes.
5. Take each question and ask the groups what they thought the correct answers should be. Allow time for different perspectives. You will find that some members will argue with every minute detail; that is okay, dialogue is the order of the day.
6. Give the preferred responses to the factual questions and lead participants in discussions of the implications of the others.

Debriefing

1. What were your feelings when you first received the questionnaire?
2. How did you react to the discussion in your subgroup?
3. How do you feel about your knowledge of history?
4. What do you see as the effect of history on today?
5. What is the implication of this activity for you in your role at school?
6. What information or skills do you believe you need to do an even better job?

ACTIVITY 5.4: BARRIERS TO CULTURAL PROFICIENCY

Entitlement is the major theme of Chapter 5, and the unaware-ness of the need to adapt is the major theme in Chapter 4. This activity is most effective when participants have completed Chapters 4 and 5.

	Skill of Facilitator		
	Low	*Moderate*	*Extensive*
Readiness of Group Beginning			
Intermediate			
Advanced			X

Purpose

To make the barriers to cultural proficiency a part of a school's planning process

Time Needed

90 minutes-2 hours

Materials

- Copies of the Barriers to Cultural Proficiency worksheet sample (Figure D5.4.1) on paper or transparencies
- A copy of the school's core values or shared values for diversity (see Activity 6.2)
- Chart paper and marking pens, or overhead projector and transparency markers

Briefing

This activity will provide you with the opportunity to apply your understanding of the sense of entitlement concept and unawareness of the need to adapt. You will also examine the relationship between our stated and unarticulated values and the implication that this has for creating change in our school. The activity will be a mix of personal and group viewpoints and experiences.

Barriers to Cultural Proficiency			
Stated Value	Unarticulated Value	Consequent Behavior	Implications for Change
Caring	We care about people as long as they meet our expectations.	Everyone does not receive fair and equitable treatment.	I need to examine my own personal prejudices and stereotypes and check my perceptions before I take an action.

Figure D5.4.1. Worksheet Example

Process

1. Distribute the school's shared values for diversity, or core values.

2. Reproduce Figure D5.4.1, leaving space below the example to add your school's values.

3. Review the meaning of *unarticulated value*. Remind participants that it is the hidden curriculum (see Activity 2.10).

4. Add your school's values in the first column. You may do this ahead of time.

5. Ask each person to spend 15 minutes making notes on the worksheet that reflect his or her individual views and perspectives.

6. Have participants form into small groups of 4 to 6 members with particular consideration to having each small group represent the diversity of the total group as much as possible.

7. Give participants 30-60 minutes to discuss each core value and complete the worksheet.

8. Request that participants post their work on a chart or onto transparencies.

9. Encourage critical review of and reflection on the responses.

Debriefing

1. What were your feelings when you first received the worksheet?

2. How did you react to the discussion in your small group?

3. How do you feel about the levels of congruence between the stated and unarticulated values?

4. What observations do you have about the "Consequent Behaviors" and "Implications for Change" columns?

5. What did you learn about your school? Your colleagues? Yourself?

6. What is the implication of this activity for you in your role at school?

7. What information or skills do you believe you need to do an even better job?

8. How will you use this information?

Variations

1. Step 6 can be done within culturally defined groups and the information shared across cultural groups.

2. This activity can be divided among groups in such a manner that each group specializes in one essential element. If you decide to use this technique, it is advisable for each group to understand that all groups will have input to one another's products.

3. Use this activity to discuss classroom or district issues.

ACTIVITY 5.5: CULTURAL PROFICIENCY
DISCUSSION STARTERS

		Skill of Facilitator		
		Low	*Moderate*	*Extensive*
Readiness of Group	Beginning			
	Intermediate			X
	Advanced			

Purpose

- To reinforce the principles of cultural proficiency
- To identify how the principles of cultural proficiency can be translated into school behavior

Time Needed

60 minutes

Materials

- Figure 2.4 (Guiding Principles)
- Cultural Proficiency Discussion Starters (Figure D5.5.1)

Briefing

Let's look at the principles of cultural proficiency to make sure we know what they mean in relationship to how we do things at this school.

Process

1. Distribute Figures 2.4 and D5.5.1.
2. Divide the group into small groups, assigning one question to each group.
3. Ask the small groups to respond to their question. Note that each question relates to a corresponding principle.
4. Reconvene the large group and share the responses, encouraging critical reflection and review.

Cultural Proficiency Discussion Starters

1. **Culture is ever present.** List aspects of culture—yours and your clients'—that affect how your message is received.

2. **People are served in varying degrees by the dominant culture.** What works for the dominant culture may not work for nondominant cultures, so consider alternatives.

3. **People have group identities and personal identities.** List some words and phrases that might insult or discount members of cultural groups in your school or district.

4. **Diversity within cultures is important.** List specific names for members of these major U.S. cultural groups:

   Asian
   Black
   Homosexual
   Hispanic
   Native American
   White

5. **Each group has unique cultural needs.** What are some of the unique cultural needs of your clients and colleagues?

Figure D5.5.1. Worksheet Sample

Debriefing

1. What happened in your small groups? How easy or difficult was it to answer the questions?

2. How do you feel about your responses?

3. Have you ever thought of parents, community, students, or one another as customers?

4. How does thinking in terms of customer or client relations alter the way you respond to these groups?

5. What are the implications for your responses?

6. How will you use this information?

Variations

1. Examine the principles from the perspective of a classroom or the district.

2. Conduct this activity with one large group, inviting discussion and responses of everyone to all the questions.

ACTIVITY 5.6: DIFFERENCES THAT MAKE A DIFFERENCE

This activity is designed to help participants assess some of the barriers to cultural proficiency in the organization.

		Skill of Facilitator		
		Low	Moderate	Extensive
Readiness of Group	Beginning			
	Intermediate		X	
	Advanced			

Purpose

To name and describe some of the differences that make a difference in our school

Time Needed

60 minutes

Materials

- One sheet of chart paper for every 4 people
- Markers for each person
- Masking tape

Briefing

Making a commitment to cultural proficiency means examining the school's climate to ascertain what goes on in the culture that may cause people to feel uncomfortable. In this activity, we are going to reflect on the differences that make a difference at our school. Think of a time that you bumped into a difference that caused discomfort for you.

Process

1. Organize the participants into groups of 4.
2. Demonstrate for the class how to divide the paper. See Figure D5.6.1.

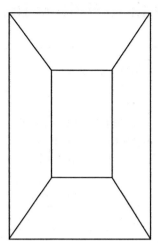

Figure D5.6.1. Handout Sample

3. Ask each participant to note in his or her portion of the diagram situations he or she has witnessed or experienced that made him or her uncomfortable.

4. After each person has written in his or her section, the 4 members of the group discuss what has been written and write a synthesis of their comments in the center of the page.

Debriefing

1. What did it feel like to name the differences that make a difference?

2. How would you categorize the differences that create problems in this school?

3. Now that you have named the differences, let's review the essential elements or the guiding principles of cultural proficiency to get some direction for addressing the issues.

Variations

1. This activity can be used to focus on just one group, department, or classroom.

2. This activity may be used as an awareness process. The group members may be comfortable just naming the issues. Deciding what to do about them can take place later in the group's process.

✦ RESOURCE E: Activities for Chapter 6 ✦

ACTIVITY 6.1: JOURNALING

During any change process, it is useful to record, in a systematic way, one's feelings and reactions. We have found journaling to be a welcome activity during intense, multiday training sessions.

		Skill of Facilitator		
		Low	*Moderate*	*Extensive*
Readiness of Group	Beginning	X		
	Intermediate			
	Advanced			

Purpose

To record your thoughts and feelings during this change process

Briefing

You are going to be hearing and experiencing things over the next few days (weeks, months) that will affect you profoundly. We want you to honor those feelings by reflecting on the experience in writing. This will give you an opportunity each day to give 100% attention to yourself.

Materials

- A blank book or a special notebook for journaling: The book should be small enough for easy carrying. Invite participants to bring their own journals if they are already journalers.

Process

1. Give participants these guidelines for their writing.
   - Each day of the training, make an entry in your journal. This is a time for you to reflect on what has happened during the day and to think about how you will make use of the experience. You may want to organize your entry as follows:

- What happened today? Specific activities, exercises, or insights that stimulated new ways of thinking—"aha's".
- How do you feel about what happened? Based on what you say at first, what are your feelings about it? Was it disturbing, energizing, a positive or negative experience?
- What are you going to do? Based on what you said happened and how you feel about it, what actions are you going to take? Consider both the short- and the long-term—tomorrow, in a few weeks, and several months from now in your work environment.

2. At the beginning of each time the group meets, ask participants to share something (not everything) from their journal entries with one other person. They may choose a different person each time.

Debriefing

1. How did you feel about being given time to journal?
2. How many have journaled before?
3. Have you ever kept a journal on a work-related process?
4. What was it like to share portions of your writing?
5. In what other setting might journaling be useful?

Variations

1. Encourage people to journal, but do not require that they share their thoughts with anyone.
2. Allow time at the end of each session for journaling.

ACTIVITY 6.2: IDENTIFYING SHARED VALUES FOR DIVERSITY

This is a good activity for Chapter 6 in that it provides participants with the opportunity to consider their individual values for diversity and to work with colleagues to determine shared values.

		Skill of Facilitator		
		Low	*Moderate*	*Extensive*
Readiness of Group	Beginning			
	Intermediate			X
	Advanced			

Purpose

- To identify the values that participants share regarding diversity
- To begin the conversation about the convergence and divergence of values
- To compare the shared values of the school with the principles of cultural proficiency

Time Needed

1-2 hours; you may want to do this in two sessions

Materials

- Pre-made chart with definition of value, shared value, and the example of a shared value
- Chart paper
- Marking pens

Briefing

We are going to identify our personal values about diversity and see if there are any values that we share.

Process

1. Post a chart in front of the room with this information:

Value: A strongly held belief that influences behavior

Shared value: A strongly held belief shared by 2 or more people

Example: Persons of all racial, ethnic, gender, socioeconomic, religious, and sexual orientation backgrounds should be treated with respect.

Clarify: A value statement is not what you believe in, but a description of what you believe. A value statement is a sentence, not a word.

Not: We believe in honesty.

But: We believe that honesty in relationships creates the foundation for conflict resolution.

2. Encourage participants to define words such as *respect* and *honesty* so they are certain they are talking about the same thing.

3. Divide participants into small groups of 3 to 5 people.

4. Have participants brainstorm a list of their individual values for diversity on chart paper or a blank transparency or chart paper.

5. Place a check mark beside those values on the list that everyone holds in common.

6. Ask each group to share its common values with the whole group.

7. Work to identify and build a consensus around the values that the entire group shares.

Debriefing

1. How difficult was it for your group to identify your shared values related to diversity?

2. What did you learn about your colleagues during the process?

3. How might the differences in values affect your relationships? Your planning?

4. What might we do with the shared values?

Variation

Use the shared values as the basis for examining work performance standards.

ACTIVITY 6.3: STRENGTH BOMBARDMENT

This is a good activity for team building. We have had success with it as an icebreaker activity with a group whose members know one another well. Also, we have had success with it as a culminating activity for groups that have been working together on a project. This activity provides for a personal focus, allows for individual expression, and facilitates discussion of similarities and differences. The activity uses positive feedback as a communication tool.

		Skill of Facilitator		
		Low	Moderate	Extensive
Readiness of Group	Beginning		X	
	Intermediate			
	Advanced			

Purpose

To build a sense of team among participants through sharing personal stories and discovering similarities and differences

Time Needed

60-90 minutes, depending on the size of the subgroups

Materials

- Strength Bombardment charts for each participant: Copy Figure E6.3.1 on one side, write the name of the participant on the reverse side of the sheet.
- Small adhesive labels, preferably colored circles about the size of a quarter (companies such as Avery and Dennison make them); if they are not available, get labels that are large enough for writing one word. Each participant should have about 10 labels for each colleague in his or her small group.

Briefing

You will be engaged in an activity in which you will describe your strengths at various times in your life and then have the opportunity to share those strengths with colleagues.

Strength Bombardment		
Age Periods	*My Accomplishments As I Define Them*	*Why They Are Important to Me*
0-10		
11-20		
21-30		
31-40		
41-50		
51-60		
61-70		

Figure E6.3.1. Worksheet Sample

Process

1. Distribute one copy of Figure E6.3.1 to each participant.

2. Ask participants to take 15 minutes to determine age periods or other important intervals in their lives (e.g., college, military, relationships, jobs), to write accomplishments (or things they have done or survived that they are proud of) for each period, and to describe why they view them as accomplishments.

3. Organize participants into groups of 3 to 6 participants. A group of 3 people will need about 30 minutes. Add 10 additional minutes of processing time for each additional member of the group.

4. In turn, each person is to summarize, in 5 minutes, his or her accomplishments and describe why he or she judges them to be accomplishments. The person is not to be interrupted during the telling of the story.

5. While the first person is telling his or her story, fellow group members are writing one-word adjectives on the labels that describe their assessment of his or her accomplishments. In

5 minutes, each group member will write on several of the labels.

6. When the first person has completed his or her story, during which time colleagues have been recording their adjectives on the label dots, he or she listens to the feedback from colleagues.

7. In turn, each colleague looks the storyteller in the eye and tells him or her what is written on each dot and alternately affixes it to the reverse side of the speaker's strength bombardment sheet. For example, "Mary, I see you as courageous, because you stood up to your brother." In just a few minutes, Mary has numerous labels on her sheet that describe her character.

8. Repeat the process for each participant.

Debriefing

1. How did you feel while telling your story?

2. What was your reaction to the feedback you received in the two forms of communication: the verbal message and direct eye contact from your colleagues and the label dots affixed to the reverse side of your sheet?

3. It never varies with this activity that someone will minimize the feedback from his or her colleagues. Some will indicate that their colleagues were generous. If this should occur, remind them that it was that person's story; the colleagues were only feeding back to that person what they were hearing.

4. Let participants know that, yes, life is not always expressed in terms of positive feedback, but it sure does feel good when it occurs.

5. What implications does this have for our work with students? With parents? With one another?

6. Invite participants to keep this sheet in a safe place and someday in the future, when things look dismal, to pull the sheet out and remind themselves of what people had to say to them on this day.

7. How were members of your group similar in their stories? Dissimilar?

ACTIVITY 6.4: THE PROCESS OF PERSONAL CHANGE

		Skill of Facilitator		
		Low	*Moderate*	*Extensive*
Readiness of Group	Beginning			
	Intermediate		X	
	Advanced			

Purpose

To raise awareness of how change takes place

Time Needed

20 minutes

Materials

- Copies of Figure E6.4.1

Briefing

We have been talking about making change, and you are probably wondering why other people have not changed yet. Let's look at the process for personal change.

Process

1. Distribute Figure E6.4.1.
2. Ask participants what they think of it.
3. Discuss the various points on Figure E6.4.1 and the movement.
4. Elicit examples from the participants for personal changes they have experienced.
5. Discuss what the process would be for someone moving toward cultural proficiency.
6. Discuss the implications for the school's or district's learning process.

Process of Personal Change

Conscious Competence

Change to Value Set B

Reinforcement

Feedback

Practice

Unconscious Competence

Reinforcement

Feedback

Practice

Behavior Change

Conscious Incompetence

Attitudinal Shift

Awareness

Unconscious Incompetence

Inappropriate Behavior

Value Set A

Figure E6.4.1 Handout Sample

Debriefing

1. What did you learn from this process? Or, what did you remember?

2. How does this process differ from how children learn?

3. What are the differences between learning something as an adult and learning something as a child?

4. How should we adapt our expectations to one another as we grow?

5. How should we adapt our expectations for our district/ school as we implement the cultural proficiency model?

Variation

Make a worksheet and have participants write their responses as they analyze a specific situation when a person or an organization went through a learning and change process.

ACTIVITY 6.5: PLANNING WITH
THE FIVE ESSENTIAL ELEMENTS

This activity is particularly effective when made an integral part of long-range or strategic planning.

		Skill of Facilitator		
		Low	*Moderate*	*Extensive*
Readiness of Group	Beginning			
	Intermediate		X	
	Advanced			

Purpose

To use the essential elements of cultural proficiency for planning

Time Needed

90 minutes to 2 hours

Materials

- Copy of Figure 2.3 (Essential Elements)
- Chart paper and markers; or blank transparencies, markers, and an overhead projector

Briefing

We are going to plan activities related to the essential elements of cultural proficiency for our school.

Process

1. Review the essential elements in Figure 2.3. Refer to Table C3.5.1 (Human Relations Needs Assessment) for examples.
2. Divide the participants into small groups of about 5 people.
3. Ask the groups to identify activities at the classroom and school level that would reinforce each element.
4. Have each group share its list.
5. Invite critical examination and revision of each list by the entire group.

Debriefing

1. How difficult was it to identify activities?
2. Were some elements more difficult than others?
3. What must happen to ensure that these activities take place?
4. If we do everything on these lists, will we be culturally proficient?
5. What else must happen?
6. How should we use the lists that we have generated? What will be our next step?
7. What is the relationship of these activities to the other things we have planned for this school?

Variations

1. Ask each group to specialize in one element.
2. Examine the school's current strategic plan and identify places where the activities generated could be incorporated.
3. Conduct this activity for specific units at the district level.

ACTIVITY 6.6: MANAGING CONFLICT
WITH OUR CORE VALUES

This activity gives participants an opportunity to anticipate and plan for resistance to change.

		Skill of Facilitator		
		Low	*Moderate*	*Extensive*
Readiness of Group	Beginning			
	Intermediate			
	Advanced			X

Purpose

To discuss the relationship of the school's core values, the elements of cultural proficiency, and managing conflict

Time Needed

60-90 minutes

Materials

- Copies of "Managing Conflict With Our Core Values" (Figure E6.6.1)
- A grid that has the same three column headings as Figure E6.6.1 but is otherwise blank. This can be on paper or on transparencies.
- Chart paper and marking pens or an overhead projector and markers
- Copies of Figure 2.3 (Essential Elements)
- A list of the school's core values

Briefing

We are going to talk about the relationship of our core values to managing conflict.

Process

1. List or distribute a list of the school's shared or core values.
2. Distribute Figure E6.6.1 and the blank grid.

	Managing Conflict With Our Core Values	
Core Values	*Relationship of Core Values to Managing Conflict*	*What I Can Say or Do to Reduce Tension and Conflict*
Quality	Unresolved conflict reduces the quality of your products.	I am concerned about the quality of the work we are doing here. Can we talk about how it can be improved?
Continuous improvement	Each time you talk through an issue, you improve the way you resolve your problems.	I know it is uncomfortable for us to talk about these things, but in the end, it really does make working together easier.
People	Without the people, we would have no business. Involve the people who are having the conflicts in resolving them.	I think we need to clear the air. Let's sit down and talk about what the real issues are.
Integrity	Acknowledge your contribution to the conflicts that arise around you.	It was not my intention to offend you. I was trying to say . . .
Teamwork	To perform together, a team needs to learn how to storm together.	Disagreements are not necessarily a bad thing. Let's each state our positions clearly. We'll decide by . . .
Customer driven	Even if you aren't bothered, if your customer is distressed, take the time to address the issues that are causing the tension.	I was not aware there was a problem. Help me understand your perceptions. Tell me what you would like from me. I am willing to . . . I am not willing to . . .
Caring	Demonstrate that you care about your colleagues by taking the time to reduce tension and problem solve together.	I am on my way to a meeting, but I do want to address these issues. Let's plan to talk at . . .
Creativity	All conflicts will not be solved the same way. Give yourself permission to go outside the box to resolve interpersonal conflicts.	Let's think about it for a day or two and see if we each can come up with at least two alternatives we both would be willing to accept.

Figure E6.6.1. Worksheet Sample

3. Ask each person to spend 15 minutes taking notes that reflect his or her individual views and perspectives regarding Figure E6.6.1.

4. Organize participants into groups of 4 to 6 members with particular consideration to having each subgroup represent the diversity of the total group as much as possible.

5. Give participants 30-60 minutes to discuss each core value as it relates to managing conflict and to complete the blank worksheet.

6. Ask participants post their work on chart paper or the transparencies.

7. Invite critical review of each group's contribution.

8. Note the similarities and differences in the small groups' products.

Debriefing

1. What were your feelings when you first received the worksheet?

2. How did you react to the discussion in your subgroup?

3. How can your incorporate the understanding of conflict you now have into your daily practice?

4. What did you learn about your school? Your colleagues? Yourself?

5. What is the implication of this activity for you in your role at school?

6. What information or skills do you believe you need to do an even better job?

7. How can we use this information?

Variations

1. Step 4 in the process can be done within culturally defined groups and the information can be shared across cultural groups.

2. Use this activity at the classroom or district level.

ACTIVITY 6.7: ORGANIZATIONAL
COMPETENCIES AND THE ESSENTIAL ELEMENTS

This activity is very useful for translating the concept of cultural proficiency into competency-based behavior.

		Skill of Facilitator		
		Low	*Moderate*	*Extensive*
Readiness of Group	Beginning			
	Intermediate			
	Advanced			X

Purpose

To identify minimal competencies for each of the essential elements

Time Needed

90 minutes-2 hours initially, plus follow-up time

Materials

- Definition of competency
- Examples of the competencies used at your school or district
- Copies of Table 6.2 (words used to describe oppressed and entitled groups)
- Copies of Figure E6.7.1 on paper or transparencies, with room to add competencies for each element
- Chart paper and marking pens or transparencies and markers
- An overhead projector

Briefing

Now that we have read and discussed this book, let's see if we can identify the competencies we use to assess performance at our school and relate them to the essential elements of cultural proficiency.

Performance Competencies and the Essential Elements	
Essential Elements	*Peformance Competency*
Values Diversity	Insists on competent staff from under represented groups.
Assesses Culture	Provides orientation to unit that includes description of the culture and the unwritten rules.
Manages Dynamics of Difference	Coaches staff and colleagues in effective language that will reduce conflict.
Institutionalizes Cultural Knowledge	Provides examples of problem situations that can be used as cases during training.
Adapts To Diversity	Holds everyone to the same standards for quality work.

Figure E6.7.1. Competency Worksheet

Process

1. Distribute the worksheets and competencies currently used to assess performance.

2. If you have to establish competencies, engage in a conversation to define what is meant by competencies for faculty, staff, and administrators. Discuss why competencies are necessary and how they are used. In some schools, competencies are implied rather than explicit.

3. Ask each person to spend 15 minutes taking notes on a worksheet noting his or her individual ideas and thoughts about competencies for each of the five elements.

4. Organize participants into subgroups of 4 to 6 members. Be sure to have each subgroup represent the diversity of the total group as much as possible.

5. Give participants 30-60 minutes to discuss each essential element and the related competencies for faculty, staff, and administrators.

6. Ask each group to present the results of its work on chart paper or transparencies.

7. Encourage critical discussion, clarification, and revision of the competencies.

Debriefing

1. What were your reactions when you first received the worksheets?
2. How did you react to the discussion in your subgroup?
3. To what extent do you think the ideas generated from all groups will be helpful in this school?
4. What did you learn about your school? Your colleagues? Yourself?
5. What is the implication of this activity for you in your role at school?
6. What information or skills do you believe you need to do an even better job?
7. How shall we use these competencies?

Variation

Have each small group specialize in just one set of competencies—faculty, staff, or administrators.

❖ RESOURCE F ❖

For Further Reading

Alvesson, M., & Per Olof, Berg. (1992). *Corporate culture and organizational symbolism.* New York: de Gruyter.

Armstrong, Thomas. (1994). *Multiple intelligences in the classroom.* Alexandria, VA: Association for Supervision and Curriculum Development.

Barth, F. (Ed.). (1991). *Ethnic groups and boundaries.* Boston: Little, Brown.

Beckhard, Richard, & Pritchard, Wendy. (1992). *Changing the essence: The art of creating and leading fundamental change in organizations.* San Francisco: Jossey-Bass.

Bennis, Warren, & Nanus, Bert. (1985). *Leaders: The strategies for taking charge.* New York: Harper & Row.

Berliner, David C. (1992, February). *Educational reform in an era of disinformation.* Paper presented to the American Association of Colleges for Teacher Education, San Antonio, TX.

Block, Peter. (1989). *The empowered manager: Positive political skills at work.* San Francisco: Jossey-Bass.

Bothwell, Lin. (1983). *The art of leadership.* New York: Prentice Hall.

Boyer, Ernest L. (1983). *High school: A report on secondary education in America.* New York: Harper & Row.

Bracey, Gerald R. (1991). Why can't they be like we were? *Phi Delta Kappan, 73*(2), 104-117.

Brookover, W. (1982). *Creating effective schools: An inservice program for enhancing school learning climate and achievement.* Holmes Beach, FL: Learning Publications.

Callahan, Raymond E. (1962). *Education and the cult of efficiency.* Chicago: University of Chicago Press.

Campbell, David. (1984). *If I'm in charge here why is everybody laughing?* Greensboro, NC: Center for Creative Leadership.

Capper, Coleen (Ed.). (1993). *Educational administration in a pluralistic society.* Albany: State University of New York Press.

Carlson, C. C., Huelskampt, Robert M., & Woodall, T. D. (1991). *Perspectives on education in America, annotated briefing—Third draft.* Alamogordo, NM: Sandia National Laboratories, Systems Analysis Department.

Chinn, Phillip C., & Gollnick, Donna M. (1994). *Multicultural education in a pluralistic society.* New York: Merrill.

Civil Rights Commission. (1971). *Mexican Americans in school: A history of educational neglect.* Washington, DC: Author.

Clark, Kenneth B., & Gordon, E. L. (1970). *Racism and American education: A dialogue and agenda for action.* New York: Harper & Row.

Comer, James P., & Haynes, N. M. (1991). Parent involvement in schools: An ecological approach. *Elementary School Journal, 3,* 271-277.

Cross, Terry L., Bazron, Barbara J., Dennis, Karl W., & Isaacs, Mareasa R. (1993). *Toward a culturally competent system of care* (Vol. 2). Washington, DC: Georgetown University Child Development Program, Child and Adolescent Service System Program.

Culbertson, J. A. (1988). A century's quest for a knowledge base. In N. J. Boyan (Ed.), *Handbook of research on educational administration.* White Plains, NY: Longman.

Davis, G., & Watson, C. (1985). *Black life in corporate America: Swimming in midstream.* Garden City, NY: Anchor.

Delpit, Lisa. (1988). The silenced dialogue: Power and pedagogy in educating other people's children. *Harvard Educational Review, 58*(3), 280-298.

Dinnerstein, Leonard, Nichols, Roger L., & Reimers, David M. (1979). *Natives and strangers: Ethnic groups and the building of America.* New York: Oxford University Press.

Edmonds, Ronald. (1979). Some schools work and more can. *Social Policy, 9*(5), 3.

Espinosa, Ruben W., & Ochoa, Alberto M. (1992). *The educational attainment of California youth: A public equity crisis.* San Diego, CA: San Diego State University, Department of Policy Studies in Language and Cross Cultural Education.

Fanon, Frantz. (1963). *The wretched of the earth.* New York: Grove.

Feldstein, S., & Costello, L. (1974). *The ordeal of assimilation: A documentary history of the white working class 1830s to the 1970s.* Garden City, NY: Anchor.

Flamholtz, Eric G., & Randle, Yvonne. (1987). *The inner game of management.* New York: American Management Association.

Francis, Dave, & Woodcock, Mike. (1990). *Unblocking organizational values.* Glenview, IL: Scott Foresman.

Franklin, John Hope. (1968). *Color and race.* Boston: Beacon.

Gardner, Neely D. (1974). *Group leadership.* Washington, DC: National Training and Development Service Press.

Giroux, Henry A. (1992). Educational leadership and the crisis of democratic government. *Educational Researcher, 21*(4), 411.

Goffman, Erving. (1959). *The presentation of self in everyday life.* New York: Doubleday.

Goodlad, John. (1983). *A place called school: Prospects for the future.* St. Louis: McGraw-Hill.

Gordon, Milton M. (1964). *Assimilation in American life: The role of race, religion, and national origins.* New York: Oxford University Press.

Greer, Colin. (1972). *The great school legend: A revisionist interpretation of American public education.* New York: Viking.

Griffiths, Daniel E. (1988). Administrative theory. In. N. J. Boyan (Ed.), *Handbook of research on educational administration.* White Plains, NY: Longman.

Guild, P., & Garger, S. (1985). *Marching to different drummers.* Alexandria, VA: Association for Supervision and Curriculum Development.

Hall, Edward T. (1959). *The silent language.* New York: Doubleday.

Hall, Edward T. (1966). *The hidden dimension.* New York: Anchor.

Hall, Edward T. (1981). *Beyond culture.* New York: Anchor.

Hall, Edward T. (1983). *The dance of life: The other dimension of time.* New York: Anchor Doubleday.

Hamada, Tomoko. (1994). *Anthropology and organizational culture.* New York: University Press of America.

Hanson, M. J., Lynch, E. W., & Wayman, K. I. (1990). Honoring the cultural diversity of families when gathering data. *Topics in Early Childhood Special Education 10*(1), 112-131.

Harragan, Betty L. (1977). *Games mother never taught you: Corporate gamesmanship for women.* New York: Warner.

Henry, Jules. (1963). *Culture against man.* New York: Vintage.

Hersey, Paul. (1984). *The situational leader.* Escondido, CA: Center for Leadership Studies.

Hersey, Paul, & Blanchard, Kenneth H. (1976). Leadership effectiveness and adaptability description. In J. W. Pfeiffer & J. E. Jones (Eds.), *1976 annual handbook for group facilitators.* San Diego, CA: University Associates.

Hilliard, Asa. (1991). Do we have the will to educate all children? *Educational Leadership, 40*(1), 31-36.

Hofstede, G. (1980). *Culture's consequences: International differences in work-related values.* Beverly Hills, CA: Sage.

Hord, Shirley M., Rutherford, William L., Huling-Austin, Leslie, & Hall, Gene E. (1987). *Taking charge of change.* Alexandria, VA: Association for Supervision and Curriculum Development.

Howe, Harold. (1991). America 2000: A bumpy ride on four trains. *Phi Delta Kappan, 73*(3), 193-203.

Immegart, Gerald L. (1988). Leadership and leadership behavior. In N. J. Boyan (Ed.), *Handbook of research on educational administration.* White Plains, NY: Longman.

Kanter, Rosabeth Moss. (1977). *Men and women of the corporation.* New York: Basic Books

Katz, Michael B. (1973). *Education in American history: Readings on the social issues.* New York: Praeger.

Knowles, Louis L., & Prewitt, K. (1969). *Institutional racism in America.* Englewood Cliffs, NJ: Prentice Hall.

Lightfoot, Sara L. (1983). *The good high school: Portraits of character and culture.* New York: Basic Books.

Loewen, James W. (1995). *Lies my teacher told me: Everything your American history textbook got wrong.* New York: New Press.

Maccoby, Michael. (1981). *The leader.* New York: Simon & Schuster.

Malinowski, Bronislaw. (1933). *A scientific theory of culture.* Chapel Hill: University of North Carolina Press.

McDermott, D., & Stadler, H. A. (1988). Attitudes of counseling students in the United States toward minority clients. *International Journal for the Advancement of Counseling, 11*(1), 61-69.

Moore, Alexander. (1992). *Cultural anthropology: The field study of human beings.* San Diego, CA: Collegiate.

Naisbitt, John. (1984). *Megatrends: Ten new directions transforming our lives.* New York: Warner.

Naisbitt, John, & Auburdene, Patricia. (1990). *Megatrends 2000: Ten new directions for the 1990's.* New York: William Morrow.

National Commission on Excellence in Education. (1983). *A nation at risk: The imperative for educational reform.* Washington, DC: Government Printing Office.

Ogbu, John U. (1992). Understanding cultural diversity and learning. *Educational Researcher, 21*(8), 5-14.

Ouchi, William G., & Wilkins, A. L. (1985). Organizational culture. *Annual Review of Sociology, 11,* 457-483.

Peters, Thomas J., & Waterman, R. H. (1982). *In search of excellence: Lessons from America's best-run companies.* New York: Harper & Row.

Pfeiffer, J. William (1987-1994). *Annuals: Developing human resources.* San Diego, CA: University Associates.

Pfeiffer, J. William, & Goodstein, L. D. (1982-1986). *Annuals for facilitators, trainers, and consultants.* San Diego, CA: University Associates.

Pfeiffer, J. William, & Jones, John E. (1972-1981). *Annual handbooks for group facilitators.* San Diego, CA: University Associates.

Pritchett, Price. (1994). *The employee handbook of new work habits for a radically changing world: Thirteen ground rules for job success in the information age.* Dallas, TX: Pritchett & Associates.

Pritchett, Price. (1995). *Culture shift: The employee handbook for changing corporate culture.* Dallas, TX: Pritchett & Associates.

Pritchett, Price, & Pound, Ron. (1991). *High velocity culture change: A handbook for managers.* Dallas, TX: Pritchett & Associates.

Pritchett, Price, & Pound, Ron. (1995). *A survival guide to the stress of organizational change.* Dallas, TX: Pritchett & Associates

Reddin, William J. (1970). *Managerial effectiveness.* New York: McGraw-Hill.

Rendon, Laura I., & Hope, Richard O., & Associates (1995). *Educating a new majority.* San Francisco: Jossey-Bass.

Richardson, Ken, & Spears, David. (1972). *Race and intelligence: The fallacies behind the race-IQ controversy.* Baltimore: Penguin.

Roberts, Wess. (1987). *Leadership secrets of Attila the Hun.* New York: Warner.

Ryan, William. (1976). *Blaming the victim.* New York: Vintage.

Sargent, Alice G. (1983). *The androgynous manager.* New York: American Management Association.

Sashkin, Marshal. (1981). An overview of ten management and organizational theorists. In W. Pfeiffer & J. Jones (Eds.), *The 1981 annual handbook for group facilitators.* San Diego, CA: University Associates.

Schien, Edgar H. (1985). *Organizational culture and leadership: A dynamic view.* San Francisco: Jossey-Bass.

Sergiovanni, Thomas J. (1991). *The principalship: A reflective practice perspective.* Boston: Allyn & Bacon.

Sergiovanni, Thomas J., & Corbally, J. E. (Eds.). (1984). *Leadership and organizational culture.* Urbana: University of Illinois Press.

Shieve, Linda T., & Schoenheit, Marian B. (1987). Leadership: Examining the elusive. *1987 yearbook of the Association for Supervision and Curriculum Development.* Alexandria, VA: Association for Supervision and Curriculum Development.

Slavin, Robert. (1990). *Cooperative learning: Theory, research and practice.* Englewood Cliffs, NJ: Prentice Hall.

Smitherman, Geneva. (1977). *Talkin and testifyin.* Boston: Houghton-Mifflin.

Tyack, David B. (1974). *The one best system: A history of American urban education.* Cambridge, MA: Harvard University Press.

Vroom, V. H., & Yetton, P. W. (1973). *Leadership and decision making.* Pittsburgh, PA: University of Pittsburgh Press.

Warren, David R. (1978). *History, education, and public policy.* Berkeley, CA: McCutchan.

Wartell, Michael A., & Huelskamp, Robert M. (1991). *Testimony of Michael A. Wartell & Robert M. Huelskamp, Sandia National Laboratories, before subcommittee on elementary, secondary, and vocational education, committee on education and Labor, U.S. House of Representatives. July 18.*

References

Adams, David Wallace. (1996). Fundamental considerations: The deep meaning of Native American schooling, 1880-1900. In T. Beauboeuf-Lafontant & D. S. Augustine (Eds.), *Facing racism in education* (2nd ed.). Cambridge, MA: Harvard University.

Argyris, Chris. (1990). *Overcoming organizational defenses: Facilitating organizational learning.* Englewood Cliffs, NJ: Prentice Hall.

Association of California School Administrators. (1991). Whites think black kids can't learn, pollster says. *EDCAL, 21*(4), 1.

Banks, James. (1994). *Multiethnic education: Theory and practice.* Needham, MA: Allyn & Bacon.

Barker, Joel (Producer). (1996). *Paradigm principles* [Video]. (Available from Charthouse International Learning Corporation, Burnsville, MN)

Barker, Joel Arthur. (1989). *Discovering the future: The business of paradigms.* Lake Elmo, MN: ILI Press.

Beckhard, Richard, & Harris, Rueben. (1987). *Organizational transitions: Managing complex change.* Addison Wesley.

Boaz, David, & Crane, Edward (Eds.). (1985). *Beyond the status quo: Policy proposals for America.* Washington, DC: Cato Institute.

Boyd, Malcolm. (1984). *Take off the masks.* Philadelphia: New Society.

Bureau of the Census. (1997). *Census updates, 1997.* Washington, DC: Author.

California Commission on Teacher Credentialing. (1995). *Standards of quality and effectiveness for administrative services credential programs.* Sacramento, CA: Author.

Cheek, Robert. (1976). *Assertive black puzzled white.* San Luis Obispo, CA: Impact.

Comer, James P. (1988). Educating poor and minority children. *Scientific American, 259*(5), 42-48.

Cross, Terry L., Bazron, Barbara J., Dennis, Karl W., & Isaacs, Mareasa R. (1989). *Toward a culturally competent system of care.* Washington, DC: Georgetown University Child Development Program, Child and Adolescent Service System Program.

Cummins, Jim. (1988). From multicultural to anti-racist education: An analysis of programmes and practices in Ontario. In T. Skuttnabb-Kangas & J. Cummins, *Minority education.* Philadelphia: Multilingual Matters.

Cummins, Jim. (1990). Empowering minority students. In N. M. Hidalgo, C. L. McDowell, & E. V. Siddle (Eds.), *Facing racism in education.* Cambridge, MA: Harvard University.

Deal, Terence, & Kennedy, Allen. (1982). *Corporate cultures: The rites and rituals of corporate life.* Reading, MA: Addison Wesley.

Delpit, Lisa. (1993). Silenced dialogue. In L. Weis & M. Fine (Eds.), *Beyond silenced voices: Class, race, and gender in United States schools.* Albany: State University of New York Press.

Delpit, Lisa, et al. (1995). *Rethinking schools: An agenda for change.* New York: New Press.

Deming, C. Edwards. (1986). *Out of the crisis: Productivity and competitive position.* Cambridge, UK: Cambridge University Press.

Drucker, Peter F. (1954). *The practice of management.* New York: Harper & Row.

Duchene, Marlys. (1990). Giant law, giant education, and ant: A story about racism and Native Americans. In N. M. Hidalgo, C. L. McDowell, & E. V. Siddle (Eds.), *Facing racism in education.* Cambridge, MA: Harvard University.

Eakin, Sybil, & Backler, Alan. (1993). *Every child can succeed: Readings for school improvement.* Bloomington, IN: Agency for Instructional Technology.

Ellison, Ralph. (1952). *Invisible man.* New York: Random House.

Fine, Michelle. (1993). Missing discourse of desire. In L. Weis & M. Fine (Eds.), *Beyond silenced voices: Class, race, and gender in United States schools.* Albany: State University of New York Press.

Franklin, John Hope, & Moss, A. A., Jr. (1988). *From slavery to freedom: A history of Negro Americans.* New York: McGraw-Hill.

Freire, Paolo. (1970). *Pedagogy of the oppressed* (Nyra Bergman Ramos, Trans.). New York: Seabury.

Fullan, Michael. (1991). *The new meaning of educational change.* New York: Teachers College Press.

Gilligan, Carol. (1983). *In a different voice.* Cambridge, MA: Harvard University Press.

Giroux, Henry. (1992). *Border crossings: Cultural workers and the politics of education.* New York: Routledge.

Harrison, Barbara Schmidt. (1992). *Managing change in organizations.* Los Angeles: Baskin-Robbins International.

Harrison, Roger, & Stokes, H. (1992). *Diagnosing organization culture.* San Diego, CA: Pfeiffer & Co.

Hawley, Willis. (1983). Strategies for effective desegregation: Lessons from research. Lexington, MA: Lexington Books.

Hodgkinson, Harold. (1991). Reform versus reality. *Phi Delta Kappan, 73*(1), 8-16.

Howard, G. R. (1993). Whites in multicultural education: Rethinking our role. *Phi Delta Kappan, 75*(1), 36-41.

Kohn, Alfie. (1998). Only for my kid: How privileged parents undermine school reform. *Phi Delta Kappan, 79,* 568-579.

Kovel, Joel. (1984). *White racism: A psychohistory.* New York: Columbia University Press.

Kozol, Jonathan. (1991). *Savage inequalities: Children in America's schools.* New York: Harper Perennial.

Ladson-Billings, Gloria. (1994). *Dreamkeepers: Successful teachers of African American children.* San Francisco: Jossey-Bass.

Levin, Henry M. (1988). *Accelerated schools for at-risk students.* New Brunswick, NJ: Center for Policy Research in Education.

Locust, Carol. (1996). Wounding the spirit: Discrimination and traditional American Indian beliefs. In T. Beauboeuf-Lafontant & D. S. Augustine (Eds.), *Facing racism in education* (2nd ed.). Cambridge, MA: Harvard University.

Massey, Morris. (1979a). *The people puzzle: Understanding yourself and others.* Reston, VA: Reston.

Massey, Morris (Producer). (1979b). *What you are is where you were when* . . . [Film]. (Available from Morris Massey Associates, Boulder, CO)

McCarthy, Cameron. (1993). After the canon: Knowledge and ideological representation in the multicultural discourse on curriculum reform. In C. McCarthy & W. Crichlow (Eds.), *Race identity and representation in education.* New York: Routledge.

McGregor, Douglas M. (1960). *The human side of enterprise.* New York: McGraw-Hill.

McIntosh, Peggy. (1988). *White privilege and male privilege: A personal account of coming to see correspondences through work in women's studies.* Wellesley, MA: Wellesley College.

Oakes, Jeannie. (1985). *Keeping track: How schools structure inequality.* New Haven, CT: Yale University Press.

Oakes, Jeannie, & Lipton, Martin. (1990). *Making the best of school.* New Haven, CT: Yale University Press.

Ogbu, John U. (1978). *Minority education and caste: The American system in cross-cultural perspective.* New York: Academic Press.

Ogbu, John U., & Matute-Bianchi, M. E. (1990). Understanding sociocultural factors: Knowledge, identity and school adjustment. In Charles

Leyba (Ed.), *Beyond language: Social and cultural factors in schooling language minority students.* Los Angeles: California State University.

Owens, Robert G. (1991). *Organizational behavior in education.* Englewood Cliffs, NJ: Prentice Hall.

Owens, Robert G. (1995). *Organizational behavior in education, 5th edition.* Needham Heights, MA: Allyn & Bacon.

Pate, Gerald S. (1988). Research on reducing prejudice. *Social Education, 52*(4), 287-289.

Ponterotto, J. G. (1988). Racial consciousness development among white counselor trainees: A stage model. *Journal of Multicultural Counseling, 16,* 146-156.

Riot Commission. (1968). *Report of the National Advisory Commission on Civil Disorders.* Washington, DC: Government Printing Office.

Rosenthal, Robert, & Jacobsen, L. (1966). Teacher expectations: Determinants of pupils IQ gains. *Psychological Abstracts, 19,* 115-118.

Sadker, Myra & Sadker, David. (1994). *Failing at fairness: How America's schools cheat girls.* New York: Charles Scribner's Sons.

Sapon-Shevin, Mara. (1993). Gifted education. In L. Weis & M. Fine (Eds.), *Beyond silenced voices: Class, race, and gender in United States schools.* Albany: State University of New York Press.

Senge, Peter, et al. (1994). *The fifth discipline fieldbook: Strategies and tools for building a learning organization.* New York: Doubleday.

Shirrts, R. Garry. (1969). *Starpower.* Del Mar, CA: Simile II.

Sizemore, Barbara, A. (1983). *An abashing anomaly: The high achieving predominately black elementary school.* Pittsburgh: Department of Black Community Education, Research and Development, University of Pittsburgh.

Sizer, Theodore. R. (1985). *Horace's compromise: The dilemma of the American high school.* Boston: Houghton Mifflin.

Slavin, Robert. (1996). *Every child, every school: Success for all.* Thousand Oaks, CA: Corwin.

Sleeter, Christine E. (Ed.). (1991). *Empowerment through multiculural education.* Albany: SUNY Press.

Sleeter, Christine E., & Grant, Carl A. (1991). Mapping terrains of power: Student cultural knowledge versus classroom knowledge. In C. E. Sleeter (Ed.), *Empowerment through multicultural education.* Albany: State University of New York Press.

Sparks, Dennis. (1997). Maintaining the faith in teachers' ability to grow: An interview with Asa Hilliard. *Journal of Staff Development, 18,* 24-5.

Suzuki, Bob. (1987). *Cultural diversity: Achieving equity through diversity.* (ERIC Document Reproduction Service No. ED303527)

Terry, Robert W. (1970). *For whites only.* Grand Rapids, MI: Eerdmans.

Valverde, Leonard A., & Brown, Frank. (1988). Influences on leadership development among racial and ethnic minorities. In N. J. Boyan

(Ed.), *Handbook of research on educational administration*. White Plains, NY: Longman.

Vigil, J. Diego. (1980). *From Indians to Chicanos: A sociocultural history*. St. Louis, MO: Mosby.

Weiss, Andrea, & Schiller, Greta. (1988). *Before Stonewall: The making of a gay and lesbian community*. Tallahassee, FL: Naiad.

West, Cornel. (1993). The new cultural politics of difference. In C. McCarthy & W. Crichlow (Eds.), *Race identity and representation in education*. New York: Routledge.

Wheatley, Margaret J. (1992). *Leadership and the new science*. San Francisco: Berrett-Koehler.

Wheelock, Anne. (1992). *Crossing the tracks: How "untracking" can save America's schools*. New York: New Press.

Wiggins, Grant. (1989). A true test: Toward more authentic and equitable assessment. *Phi Delta Kappan, 71,* 703-719.

Willis, Arlette Ingram. (1996). Reading the world of school literacy: Contextualizing the experience of a young African American male. In T. Beauboeuf-Lafontant & D. S. Augustine (Eds.), *Facing racism in education* (2nd ed.). Cambridge, MA: Harvard University.

Wright, Richard. (1940). *Native son*. New York: Harper & Row.

Index